Spiritual Hospital Manual

Deborah Nembhard-Colquhoun

SPIRITUAL HOSPITAL MANUAL
Copyright © 2016 by Deborah Nembhard-Colquhoun

All rights reserved. Neither this publication nor any part of this publication may be reproduced or transmitted in any form or by any means, electronic or mechanical, including photocopying, recording or any information storage and retrieval system, without permission in writing from the author.

This book is intended to provide helpful information on the subjects discussed, and is not a substitution for medical advice. As in all matters of health, please consult a physician before undertaking any changes to diet, exercise, and medication.

Any resources referred to throughout the manual are offered as suggested resources only. These resources are not intended in any way to be or imply an endorsement on the part of Spiritual Hospital, nor can we vouch for their accuracy.

Scripture quotations marked KJV are taken from the Holy Bible, King James Version, which is in the public domain. Scripture quotations marked NIV are taken from the Holy Bible, NEW INTERNATIONAL VERSION®. Copyright © 1973, 1978, 1984, 2011 by Biblica, Inc. All rights reserved worldwide. Used by permission. NEW INTERNATIONAL VERSION® and NIV® are registered trademarks of Biblica, Inc. Use of either trademark for the offering of goods or services requires the prior written consent of Biblica US, Inc. Scripture quotations marked NKJV are taken from the New King James Version®. Copyright © 1982 by Thomas Nelson, Inc. Used by permission. All rights reserved. Scripture quotations marked NASB are taken from the New American Standard Bible®, Copyright © 1960, 1962, 1963, 1968, 1971, 1972, 1973, 1975, 1977, 1995 by The Lockman Foundation. Used by permission.

ISBN: 978-1-4866-1402-8   Printed in Canada

Word Alive Press
131 Cordite Road, Winnipeg, MB R3W 1S1
www.wordalivepress.ca

Library and Archives Canada Cataloguing in Publication

Nembhard-Colquhoun, Deborah, author
    Spiritual hospital manual : providing hope / Deborah Nembhard-Colquhoun.

Issued in print and electronic formats.
ISBN 978-1-4866-1402-8 (paperback).--ISBN 978-1-4866-1403-5 (ebook)

    1. Spiritual life--Christianity. 2. Spiritual healing--Christianity.
3. Diseases--Religious aspects--Christianity. I. Title.

BV4501.3.N36 2016   248.4   C2016-906497-2
                                                  C2016-906498-0

CONTENTS

	Acknowledgments	v
	Spiritual Hospital Manual: Providing Hope	vii
	The History of Spiritual Hospital	ix
	Introduction	xi
1.	Human Disconnection from and Provision Back to the Spiritual Source	1
2.	Simple Spiritual Characteristics That We Can Identify in the Natural	3
3.	Human Eternal Life/Exit to the Spiritual Realm	9
4.	The Good and Bad Side of the Supernatural	13
5.	Our Protection from the Enemy	21
6.	Laws in the Spiritual That Dictate the Natural	23
7.	Spiritual Warfare: Secrets of the Enemy!	29
8.	Why Is There a Need for a Spiritual Hospital?	39
9.	The Supernatural God Wants Us Healed	43
10.	How We Conduct Procedures for Spiritual Sickness	47
11.	Spiritual Medication—The Two Best Ones on the Market	53
12.	Departments That Aid in One's Well-being	55
13.	How Do We Raise the Dead?	63
14.	We Must Follow Christ	67
15.	All Believers Are Given Spiritual Power	69
16.	Healing and Deliverance	79

17.	Spiritual Covering	83
18.	The Power of Praise and Worship	89
19.	General Tips to Live a Fulfilled Life	93
20.	Ministry Information	95
21.	Encouraging Mini-Sermons	97
22.	Identifying a Cult Church	147
23.	Teaching Outline for Baby Christians	151

ACKNOWLEDGMENTS

Special acknowledgment to my husband and partner in ministry, Pastor Wilkie Colquhoun—an example of a true man of God.

Bro. David McFarlane—a humble man of God. Thank you for the tremendous work in editing this book.

Margaret Hardat, Minister Rona De La Rosa, Sis Marina Mungal, and Tina Motion—I call you faithful. You stood by my side through thick and thin.

Bishop Pat Johnson—a humble servant of God who is after God's own heart. You have done more and beyond for Spiritual Hospital.

Minister Diane Earle—God bless you in your obedience of lifting up my hands in ministry.

Thank you also to Pastor David Duncan and Minister Tess Bastca.

To all the members, friends, and visitors of Spiritual Hospital—you caused me to want to go on. How could I have done it without you? God bless you all!

SPIRITUAL HOSPITAL MANUAL: PROVIDING HOPE

Spiritual Hospital ministry strategies, formulas, interventions, healing and deliverance, spiritual directives, tools for encouraging and building awareness, exposing the dark side of the spiritual, resources ... all in a book.

You have tried everything, including the medical system, and still can't find help. You might be wondering if you'll ever be healed or delivered. Did you know that some sicknesses are spiritual and cannot be healed with medical intervention?

You may feel like all hope is gone and that life has no meaning, or that you're in a spiritual prison—oppressed, perplexed, and depressed. This book could be the answer for you. If doctors have given you up to die, you can be healed. It doesn't matter how bad the issue is, you can be healed. There is a sovereign power that is substantially greater than any human knowledge, wisdom, or prescription. God specializes in healing all things. Let's find out how you can be healed spiritually, physically, emotionally, financially, and relationally.

Science and medicine accomplish great things, and they are certainly a gift from God that He uses to bring healing and deliverance. However, there is also a spiritual solution for everyone, but people are perishing because of lack of knowledge (Hosea 4:6). This book will not only enhance your spiritual knowledge, but educate you about the Word of God over your life. This book will also show you how to apply biblical principles in order for the full manifestation of healing to take place.

THE HISTORY OF SPIRITUAL HOSPITAL

Before I founded Spiritual Hospital, I met with God spiritually at a young age. I later developed a very close relationship with God, and my love for Him increased. He speaks to me in several ways, and to be honest, I often ignored His voice.

In 2009, I felt a strong burden to pursue studies at Bible college. I also obeyed God's voice when He directed me to start an evangelism ministry in the Toronto area. God began opening doors for me to proclaim the Gospel; we saw the miracles of His providence, power, and protection in the lives of those to whom we witnessed. Travelling from church to church, we soon discovered that many Christians were in need of spiritual healing and deliverance. Unable to rest with this burden, I went to God in prayer and cried out over the condition of the people. I asked God to raise up someone who would be a channel He could use to heal and deliver—having no idea that person would be me. Being an intercessor, I went through a spiritual birthing process, similar to that which a pregnant woman would go through in the natural world. God's desires became my desires. I often felt as though He had placed His heart inside of me; it was broken, touched with people's infirmities and burdens. I couldn't be at ease until something was done.

This ministry has extended into a church called Spiritual Hospital. In the beginning, we didn't know about all the tremendous plans God had for His ministry, yet we are here today as a testimony to the sovereign plan of God, serving as representatives of what God can do with those who are willing.

Deborah Nembhard-Colquhoun

It's been just over two years since we launched the Spiritual Hospital. Many have come and received healing and deliverance and returned to their churches, while others have stayed. Through the power of God, we have seen many come to accept Jesus Christ as their personal Lord and Saviour for the first time, including Hindus, Muslims, and Satan worshippers. God has opened the door for Spiritual Hospital to be on television, where we reach a large audience within Canada. We're in the process of launching our TV ministry worldwide. To God be all the glory!

Without a shadow of a doubt, Spiritual Hospital was birthed for God's purposes. We are only vessels of God, and it's so amazing to see how He connects people with like hearts and spirits, allowing individuals to come and go according to His plan. I am confident that God is with us; therefore, no one can be against us. We are indeed on a journey of great and awesome endeavours.

INTRODUCTION

Every human being was created to prosper in all areas of their life and to be in good health; therefore, if one is not walking in complete prosperity and health, something is not as it was intended to be. Most people experience some kind of emotional, mental, sociological, or physiological dilemma without any understanding of how to be free. Poverty, curses, and sicknesses are rampant in the lives of many in our society. Even if we had all the material resources we needed and were living healthy lives, we would still need to understand the void we often experience.

Many people seek different means of help, including the medical system, materialistic aid, and even a type of spiritual aid, yet they end up without answers. This void can only be filled by spiritual means ... but how? Having a good understanding of the spiritual realm will help us deal with the many predicaments and questions outlined above. Although we were born with a human nature, we were also born with a spiritual side. Many people refuse to think of the spiritual, because it's believed that the spiritual realm exists somewhere out in space, and that it's something unreachable. However, the spiritual realm is very real and attainable—it's just in a different dimension.

I once heard someone say, "As it is in the natural, so it is in the spiritual." This statement is somewhat true. From the human point of view, the spiritual is not easily comprehended, but there is no limit to the spiritual realm. It's operating right here on Earth, so close that it even exists within our hearts. It's difficult to comprehend, though, because we can't see it with our natural eyes. The natural man can't understand the things of the spirit, because it is foolishness to him. It takes much faith to understand the spiritual. Before we go any further, I'd like to point out that the spiritual is the same as the supernatural.

In this manual, we'll cover several supernatural methods that will aid individuals seeking to be healed and delivered from many sicknesses that science and medicine cannot heal. In a nutshell, one will discover insights they can apply to find guidance for their life, and healing in mind, body, and spirit.

What Is the Difference between the Natural and the Spiritual?

Like the natural, the spiritual is very functional. Activities take place there on an ongoing basis; it's structured with authority, laws, rules, and regulations. There is a power of good and evil that exists there. We can't compare the natural to the spiritual; rather, we can say that the natural is a poor image, or shadow, of the spiritual. Everything arises from the spiritual; the natural is even subject to the spiritual, but the spiritual is not subject to the natural. The components of Earth are controlled by the mechanisms of the spiritual. In the natural, we have knowledge, wisdom, and intellect. The same elements exist in the spiritual, but they are absolute, infinite, and eternal. Events that take place in both the spiritual and the natural realms always affect each other; however, spiritual occurrences determine what takes place in the natural. The natural and the spiritual are interfaced, but we cannot see this.

As it is in the natural, so it is in the spiritual. Take an automobile, for example. It's manufactured and needs oil, gas, and maintenance in order to operate properly. To survive as created beings, we also need a natural and spiritual life source. People are aware of the natural source, but not the spiritual source, which is the supernatural. Could that source be God? We will find out later. Believe it or not, we also need supernatural fuel and maintenance, supernatural medication and food, and supernatural doctors. Although mankind was born with a human side, we were also born with a spiritual side and were given supernatural features and capabilities.

1. HUMAN DISCONNECTION FROM AND PROVISION BACK TO THE SPIRITUAL SOURCE

From the beginning, we were created to live a fulfilled life and nothing else. If this is the case, then what went wrong? It all started at the beginning of creation. The Bible says that God created humans in His own image (spiritual). We were once perfect, but we allowed our flesh (the natural) to dominate and cause us to sin against God. As a result, we malfunctioned and were spiritually separated from God, leaving us with a feeling of emptiness, or a void, that created in us a desire to seek fulfillment. This void is a real need to connect to the one true source, our maker, God, and the supernatural.

When mankind originally sinned, they were spiritually cut off from the supernatural life source. We might be able to function in the supernatural at times, but only because of a spiritual counterfeit source. This counterfeit source might have some temporary benefits; however, without the true source (God), it is useless. We might think that we're OK, but we're not, especially for eternity. Without God we're nothing but humans living as malfunctioning beings in a dysfunctional world. We're like fish out of water, struggling to live a life in the right environment. Why do you think we're susceptible to disease, pain, sin, and death? Why do you think our bodies will die? Despite such tragedy, God has provided a means for us to be in the original environment and be connected to the source of all things (God).

John 3:16 says, "*For God so loved the world, that he gave His only begotten Son, that whosoever believeth in Him should not perish, but have everlasting life.*" It's God's will that we prosper and be in good health.

"*Beloved, I wish above all things that thou mayest prosper and be in health, even as thy soul prospereth*" (3 John 1:2). It's the enemy who placed humans in this dilemma, and he's still trying hard to keep us in misery. God, on the other hand, desires the best for us. John 10:10 says, "*The thief cometh not, but for to steal, and to kill, and to destroy: I am come that they might have life, and that they might have it more abundantly.*" He sent Jesus, the only true sacrifice, to redeem us back to Him and the original life He planned for us.

God isn't pleased when we don't prosper, because it's His will for us to prosper. He created everything in the spiritual realm, and He also prepared ways by which we are to obtain what He created for us. Everything we ever needed to know about our prosperity is in the Bible. This book, the Word of God, is not an ordinary book—it's a divine, spiritual manual prepared and provided by God so that we can have access to spiritual things while we are here in the natural. But are we reading it? If so, do we understand what we are reading? Do we believe it?

> *For the word of God is quick, and powerful, and sharper than any two-edged sword, piercing even to the dividing asunder soul and spirit, and the joints and marrow, and is a discerner of the thoughts and intents of the heart.*
>
> —Hebrews 4:12

The Bible is God's spiritual way of talking to us so that we can comprehend spiritual things with our finite minds. God wants us to be seated in heavenly places while we are here on Earth. He desires for us to have not only complete joy, peace, and happiness, but also assurance for eternity. If we are Christians who are born again of the Spirit of God, we have the key; we have access to all the power of the spiritual.

2. SIMPLE SPIRITUAL CHARACTERISTICS THAT WE CAN IDENTIFY IN THE NATURAL

Do you know that trees, stones, energy, wind, time, gravity, space, love, and your thoughts are immaterial things? We comprehend the reality of the spiritual by recognizing the immaterial forces that are in our lives.

Whether or not we want to believe that the spiritual exists, it does. Among its many proofs is that all humans operate to some extent in the spiritual. For example, love is spiritual, yet it influences people in the natural through the bonds of friendship, family relationships, culture, and race. We're able to feel and convey love; we're able to experience joy, peace, and hate. These are all products of the spiritual. Our inadequacy to function in the spiritual realm is a result of our original fall in the Garden of Eden. Humans were created to have a great amount of authority within the spiritual world, but they allowed Satan to deprive them of this privilege. Unbelief is a great spiritual blockage that the enemy uses to stop people from fulfilling their spiritual privilege. You might ask if unbelief is a natural thing, and the answer is no!

Everything That Is in the Natural Is a By-Product of the Supernatural

Let's look at love, which is one of the most important elements of the Christian walk. Love manifests itself in the natural, but is a by-product of the supernatural. Anything that can't be produced in the natural or by the natural is from the spiritual; therefore, love is from the supernatural. Can you produce love? You might think that you can, but you can't. You can only use what has already been created, but you can store and give as much as you can. Not only is love the source of the supernatural God, it is the chief nature of God. Can we see love? No, we only see the evidence of love in action.

Love is powerful! It's one of the most powerful weapons on Earth to conquer a multitude of sins, destroy hate/rage, seek the needy, the hurting, and the lonely, and win the unsaved for Christ. If you have God's love, it will manifest in you and make you an instrument of love. In the last days, God will pour out His love into this dry and thirsty land (His people), which will spring forth into new life. The love of God is like the sun; it covers everything in your life. People don't know how much Christ loves them, because Christians are not showing love. When the world sees love being poured out, they will see the love of God. How do you show love? You use your hands, your feet, and your mouth. You can't fight love. You just have to accept it, because even if it's rejected, it will just keep coming back. When we have the love of God in us, we don't just love certain people ... we love everyone, even the unlovable. God's love goes beyond all barriers, so go out of your way to love people. Every attack against you is an opportunity to show God's love and favour.

Many of the attributes exhibited in the natural are not natural. In addition to love, let's take a look at righteousness. Righteousness can become a natural part of us, but we can't produce righteousness on our own. Righteousness is from the spiritual, just as love is from the spiritual. God imputes these attributes to us from Himself (Romans 1:17).

Human beings exist in the natural, yet they are a product of the spiritual. The clothing we wear is from the natural. But is clothing really from the natural? No, everything that exists is a product of the supernatural. Bet you never thought of that one! Think about it for a moment... beyond the manufacturing plant, where did the material that produces clothing really come from? The entire world and its elements came into being by someone, and that someone is completely supernatural (God). Nothing that is in the natural existed before creation. Things could not just exist or come into being by themselves. God is the source of all things, and He created everything. Our resources are products of the spiritual; therefore, the very clothing we wear came from the supernatural. Our clothing is only natural because it exists in the natural. Humans use the product(s) that God created to create our own designs. If you want to take it even further, the very knowledge and creativity that was used in the process of manufacturing are a product of the supernatural, because they came from God.

Over the centuries, geniuses have tried to produce humans, but they will never be successful, because all the details of human beings came from the supernatural. All the secret ingredients for creating humans are in the hands of God, and He will never give away that secret to anyone. Geniuses might as well continue to create lifeless creatures. Since they are such geniuses, why don't they create an original living being themselves instead of trying to think the thoughts of the supernatural God of creation? I guess they are only limited to the natural. How genius are they here? I guess not much.

Who is the best person to fix a product? Wouldn't you think it's the one who created it? I would think so, because they know all the elements of the product and its functions. Then why do people put their trust in imitators? We applaud the knowledge that God has given doctors, and we also encourage people to seek out natural physicians; however, our focus at Spiritual Hospital is on the one who created all mankind—the great physician, Doctor Jesus. Not only has He made provision to repair mankind, but He has left directives for believers and has also empowered them to fix His malfunctioning humans. Why are there so many sick and hurting people? Could it be because people are lacking spiritual knowledge?

How Can One Perceive the Spiritual in the Natural?

Although we are spiritual beings, a large percentage of our spiritual part is being shut down. We tend to operate with logic and reasoning rather than with spiritual ability. So how can we perceive the spiritual? Let's face it, for you to understand the spiritual, it must be explained in the natural. Explaining it outside of our human comprehension wouldn't make sense, and it wouldn't be understood. Those in the medical field are quick to rule out everything else and will diagnose you as being mentally unstable if you tell them about your experiences outside of the natural. There are many references I could give to explain how the natural is like the spiritual; however, these scriptures will explain it best:

> *Philip saith unto him, Lord, show us the Father, and it sufficeth us. Jesus saith unto him, Have I been so long time with you, and yet hast thou not known me, Philip? He that hath seen me hath seen the Father; and how sayest thou then, Show us the Father? Believest thou not that I am in the Father, and the Father in me? The words that I speak unto you I speak not of myself: but the Father that dwelleth in me, he doeth the works. Believe me that I am in the Father, and the Father in me: or else believe me for the very works' sake.*
> —John 14:8-11

God came all the way from Heaven and manifested Himself so that we could comprehend the supernatural God, yet we are still questioning. All the attributes Jesus exhibited, such as miraculous works, signs, and wonders, were all products of the supernatural. Jesus is called *"the image of the invisible God"* (Colossians 1:15). Like it is in the natural, so it is in the supernatural. We aren't able to see God, as He is supernatural. While Christ was on Earth, however, we could see God through Christ. The supernatural God took flesh upon Himself so that He could redeem human beings back unto Himself, and so that we could also see the supernatural God.

The Gospel of John defined it as follows: *"... the Word was with God, and the Word was God"* (1:1). He goes on to say that:

> *... the Word was made flesh, and dwelt among us, (and we beheld his glory, the glory as of the only begotten of the Father,) full of grace and truth ... no man hath seen God at any time, the only begotten Son, which is in the bosom of the Father, he hath declared him."*
> —John 1:14, 18

God is supernatural (spirit), and only the spiritual side of humans can truly know God. This side must be restored to a level of spiritual consciousness. God has provided the means to achieve this, but we have to believe so that the Holy Spirit will enter our mortal bodies and reveal to us the knowledge of God. This is why Christians are different from the unsaved—they have had a spiritual transformation, and the things of the spirit have become as clear as day to them, while the unsaved are blind to the truth.

3. HUMAN ETERNAL LIFE/EXIT TO THE SPIRITUAL REALM

People doubt the existence of the spiritual realm; however, sooner or later this fact will become a reality for all humans, because all of us will have to go to this world when we die. The Word of God declares, "... *it is appointed unto men once to die, but after this the judgment* ..." (Hebrews 9:27). Regardless of technology, medicine, medical intervention, or science, humans will die. Since Bible times, there are no records of people living over 150 years of age. All humans die, and there is nothing anyone can do about it.

Dying in the natural is just the beginning of our lives, because there is a spiritual side to everyone. Upon death, every human is dead in the flesh; however, they begin their spiritual life that will last for eternity. The spirit and soul can never die. We'll all have to live in a spiritual world, either Heaven or Hell, whether we like it or not. Our response to God's offer of salvation will determine where we end up. If we reject it, we will go to Hell for eternity, and it will be our own fault. God has provided us with enough descriptions of this horrible place called Hell. He has also announced the free gift of salvation through different means, such as the Bible, media, and the preaching of the Gospel. He also alerts our conscience to the facts of Hell, everlasting life, and His provision. God has given everyone a choice!

We are without excuse: "*And this Gospel of the kingdom shall be preached in all the world for a witness unto all nations; and then shall the end come,*" (Matthew 24:14).

For the wrath of God is revealed from heaven against all ungodliness and unrighteousness of men, who hold the truth in unrighteousness; Because that which may be known of God is manifest in them; for God hath shewed it unto them. For the invisible things of him from the creation of the world are clearly seen, being understood by the things that are made, even his eternal power and Godhead; so that they are without excuse: Because that, when they knew God, they glorified him not as God, neither were thankful; but became vain in their imaginations, and their foolish heart was darkened. Professing themselves to be wise, they became fools, and changed the glory of the uncorruptible God into an image made like to corruptible man, and to birds, and four-footed beasts, and creeping things.
—Romans 1:18-23

According to Psalm 19, God's handiwork speaks for itself and provides evidence of a supernatural creator. This theme is repeated throughout scripture:

For when the Gentiles, which have not the law, do by nature the things contained in the law, these, having not the law, are a law unto themselves: Which shew the work of the law written in their hearts, their conscience also bearing witness, and their thoughts the mean while accusing or else excusing one another.
—Romans 2:14-15

"In him was life; and the life was the light of men," (John 1:4); "*If we confess our sins, he is faithful and just to forgive us our sins, and to cleanse us from all unrighteousness,*" (1 John 1:9); "*For God so loved the world, that he gave his only begotten Son, that whosoever believeth in him should not perish, but have everlasting life,*" (John 3:16); "*The fool hath said in his heart, there is no God. Corrupt are they ...*" (Psalms 53:1)

Supernatural Mysteries at One's Death-Bed
There is a mystery in the spiritual world into which some people gain insight on their death-bed. Many people who are close to death after a

long period of suffering report that they see their loved ones and relatives who have already passed away. These dead relatives communicate with them and tell them past truths and things about the spiritual realm that would marvel anyone. We've heard of countless people who have had near death experiences and came back with many testimonies of the spiritual side. Isn't it strange to see so many people with similar experiences? For those who understand the spiritual side, it's not strange at all. This is a piece of evidence that supports the argument that all humans are spiritual.

All people were born from the spiritual world, and everyone is going to travel through a spiritual portal. Upon death, we return to our original place, but maybe to a different spiritual country, Heaven or Hell. Through death we learn that the only thing separating us from the spiritual is our human bodies. Upon death, this robe of flesh is shredded and we immediately tunnel through the spiritual realm to our spiritual destination. No wonder the Bible tells us that at this point, all Christians will leave this world and be changed from corruptible to incorruptible, from mortal to immortality.

> *Behold, I shew you a mystery; We shall not all sleep, but we shall all be changed, in a moment, in the twinkling of an eye, at the last trump: for the trumpet shall sound, and the dead shall be raised incorruptible, and we shall be changed. For this corruptible must put on incorruption, and this mortal must put on immortality. So when this corruptible shall have put on incorruption, and this mortal shall have put on immortality, then shall be brought to pass the saying that is written, Death is swallowed up in victory.*
> —1 Corinthians 15:51-54

It's impossible for human flesh to enter into this spiritual destination, never mind live there permanently, as everything there is spiritual. In this light, we can see that because we are in the flesh, we are limited to the natural. The word "natural" expresses limitation, but the word "spiritual" expresses limitlessness. In the flesh we can only do so much, live so long, and comprehend so much. We're just simple, finite beings. In the spirit, we have endless possibilities, unlimited knowledge and power, and eternal life. We will be supernatural.

4. THE GOOD AND BAD SIDE OF THE SUPERNATURAL

The Dark Side of the Spiritual

EVERYTHING ON THE DARK SIDE OF THE SPIRITUAL IS DERIVED FROM SATAN; it's a counterfeit of the good side of the spiritual. The dark side functions similarly to the good side, except in a perverse manner. Like Christians who work through the Spirit of God, wicked people work through the spirit of Satan. They are able to access the spiritual realm through a variety of means. Prayer and the Word of God are two of the weapons Satan worshippers use to war against people. How they are able to do this is beyond me, but I believe they twist the scriptures to suit their desires.

God is the source of all power, whether that power is intended for good or evil. Anything outside of God's source is useless. Christians are able to enter the spiritual realm through the sacrificial blood of the Lamb of God (Jesus Christ). In the past, sin separated us from the supernatural, from God. The shedding of blood is the only substitute for sin. Natural blood sacrifice was a temporary means to cover sin: *"... without shedding of blood is no remission,"* (Hebrews 9:22). God doesn't require any other sacrifice from us, because Jesus is the ultimate and perfect sacrifice. Jesus is *"... the Lamb of God, which taketh away the sin of the world,"* (John 1:29).

Wicked people are able to enter the spiritual realm by offering sacrifices to Satan. These sacrifices can involve the killing of animals, or even in extreme cases the killing of a human in which the blood from the sacrifice is offered up to Satan in worship. Did you know that Satan has agents working in almost every aspect of humanity? Even in hospitals he uses certain people to do destructive things. With the help of Satan and his demons, people are able to access the spiritual world, except they are limited to only the dark side of the spiritual realm. Here they can look through the eyes of Satan and see what is happening in the affairs of humans. Satan is not omnipresent, which is why he uses demonic angels to conduct wicked tasks around the world. Without any ritual or sacrifices, humans can also access the supernatural by being vessels available for Satan to use. Just like Christians, evil people also pray and fast, and worship and praise their lord, Satan. They even go beyond some Christians by conducting certain rituals, like chanting and meditation, in order to enter the spiritual realm.

Since we launched Spiritual Hospital, many people have come on an assignment from Satan to destroy us and the ministry, but they were not successful. It appears as though they were no match for us. How could they be when we are mighty in Christ ... not to mention when God and His angels are on our side?

Recently, a satanic bishop came to our church, pretending to want deliverance from his current state, and tried to use sly deception to destroy us. He used our kindness to his advantage and tried to control what was happening in our church. A lot of destruction could have been done, but he was exposed. God allowed him to tarry for a short time so that He could expose the dark side, which gave us a lot of knowledge on how the devil operates. He foolishly revealed many secrets to us that we can use to our advantage.

The bishop came as a raggedy, hungry, homeless man, claiming that he'd never received fatherly love. He said that he was sick with over fifteen diseases, and the doctors had given him up to die. This is indeed a good candidate for Spiritual Hospital. We started the process of getting him off the street, which he rejected. We placed him in a hotel temporarily, which he loved. He was given food and clothing. We worked out a plan with a government social worker to assist him financially, because we were limited in our resources. Many of the diseases started to heal. The heart issue vanished, the foot he was to have amputated was restored to health, and the one eye that was blind since birth, opened. He started singing praises and stating that God was better than Satan, and that we were treating him well. He called me "Mom" and my husband, "Father." The hospital where he was being treated called us and asked to speak to his parents (us). We purchased a Bible for him, and he seemed to be reading it faithfully. He would come to the church two hours before service, and if he couldn't go in before everyone else, he would be mad. He seemed so committed to changing his life. Isn't this a good Christian candidate? At least that's how it seemed. This is only a synopsis. He could have fooled anyone.

The Bible warns us of wolves in sheep's clothing. We need to understand that the devil doesn't come looking like the creatures in horror movies, with horns, a red fiery face, and swords, but rather he comes disguised. I caught the bishop a few times doing spells in the church; I stopped him and told him that if he did it again, he would be asked to leave. He was shocked and didn't understand how I could know what was being done. I guess he'd underestimated me. My hope was that he would truly turn from being a satanic priest. He didn't understand our power and authority in Christ, that we weren't afraid of any demons, and that our desire was to help everyone who wanted help. Apparently, he didn't want help. I believe that some people are totally sold out to the devil, just as some Christians are totally sold out to God.

His intention was not ours. We wanted to help him, but his assignment was to destroy us. He knew that and was playing on our sympathy. But if God is for us, who can be against us? What is in the dark must be exposed to the light, and as we are the light of Christ, we will see the result of the exposure. He wanted to be at the church before everyone else so that he could cast his spells.

One Thursday night, my husband, Pastor Wilkie, placed his hands on him and started praying. Astonishingly, a monstrous face manifested itself right before our eyes. His head shook violently and then turned backwards. His eyes rolled upwards, he was speaking with a strange voice, and his hands tried to fold together to form a bridge to gain power. Before that could happen, the power of God pushed him off the chair to the ground. My husband commanded the demon to leave and go back to Hell, but the demon replied that he was there on assignment. With the authority and power of God flowing through him, my husband asked the bishop about his assignment. To our surprise, everything was revealed. Unfortunately, his work had already started to have some visible effects, so thank God he was exposed before more damage was done.

I'm only sharing a little bit of the work that the satanic bishop did at Spiritual Hospital. Throughout this book, I share what I've learned about how Satan works. The satanic bishop exposed many strategies of Satan. He said that he cannot touch Christians who are strong and wear the whole armour of God, but he can influence weak Christians. He looks for an opening in individuals through which he can attack.

While he was attending church services, he would pretend to be sleeping while he communicated with evil spirits. They would whisper in the ears of individuals and tell them to hate the sister beside them. Demons caused confusion in the service and put people to sleep. They cast spells on people and afflicted them with sicknesses. I asked how he was able to afflict sickness on people, and he told me that he would form a bridge by holding hands with or touching someone, producing a mode of transfer. He also silently used certain words to cast his spells and send a spirit inside an individual. He placed a spiritual padlock on the front door so that no one would come inside or have a desire to come to the church.

How can this happen if we are of God? Well, he was using the legal rights that I gave him to be at the church. He'd announced that he was a satanic bishop, and I allowed him to be there. He was also using the spirit of the python [Satan] through the weak people to suck the life out of me, so I had no desire to pray or read the Word. Satan knows who doesn't put on the whole armour of God, and they become easy prey for him.

He revealed that there were over six hundred demons working in and through him. When casting his spells, he would communicate with these spirits, silently speaking in a demonic tongue, using sign language, and moving his hands, feet, head, and body in a certain direction. He would get very busy during healing and deliverance time, as he was actively working to prevent healing and deliverance from taking place. He told us that during one service when one of my pastors had almost delivered a person, he used a spell to block the pastor.

Satan is bold, but foolish. The satanic bishop said he was shocked by the power we had, which was the power of God, yet he came to challenge us. Didn't he know that sooner or later he would be defeated? No power can stand against God's power and win. We as believers must be aware of Satan's devices. He is not more powerful than God, but he will defeat us if we aren't alert.

After the satanic bishop came back to the natural world from the spiritual world, he didn't remember anything that had taken place, or that he had revealed the secret. This was the end of his assignment; we told him to leave. He tried to use mind manipulation on us so that we would have more sympathy on him and let him stay, but it didn't work. He even tried to counter attack us from the outside, but we anticipated this move and were prepared. We've had many similar cases to his in which people actually received their deliverance through our ministry, but he was not that case. His job was to destroy.

How can anyone sell themselves out to the devil and an eternity in Hell? There is nothing good about Satan; he is more than 100 per cent pure evil! He will use the good to lure his prey and bring pain and destruction to his victims, which may also include his closest servants. His nature is evil. You cannot bargain with Satan, and there is nothing you can do to make him change his mind. Hell is his kingdom with all of its darkness, extreme fear, pain, sorrow, wickedness, and torment. God has allowed Satan to be loose for this physical time, but soon he will be confined to Hell for eternity, along with the people here on Earth who are part of his kingdom. Why would anyone want to be part of this evil kingdom? They would have to be completely turned over to Satan.

The Good Side of the Supernatural/Christian's Eternal Home

With a revelation from God, Christians can see into both Heaven and Hell. After his death on the cross, Jesus went to Hell and conquered death for us. We no longer have to be dead spiritually (meaning to be in eternal Hell), because salvation was provided for us. Jesus took back the keys that Satan had stolen from us. Jesus says in Revelation 1:18:

"*I am he that liveth, and was dead; and, behold, I am alive for evermore, Amen; and have the keys of hell and of death.*" Jesus was dead physically, but rose with a new body that enabled Him to access and live in this spiritual realm. Like Jesus, Christians are able to see the wickedness of the enemy and use the power and authority that God provides to enter into the spiritual realm where Satan and his demons operate. Not only do we have the ability to raise war against our enemies, but we are equipped to conquer them. We have the supernatural power we need.

Heaven is the spiritual realm where God dwells; here you will find absolutely no evil. It's the realm where the source of everything and everyone originated. The only true description of Heaven is found in the Word of God; every other description is just a guess. The finite mind of a human being can't comprehend it; therefore, God gave us a description of Heaven that we can understand.

According to Scripture, Heaven can only be described as breathtaking. Oh, the splendours of Heaven will never cease! In Heaven, gold serves as the asphalt on the streets. We can't even imagine what our dwelling will be like. It must be magnificent, since Jesus is there preparing it for us. This new eternal destination will be much better than the original Garden of Eden that we were locked out of because of our sin. Heaven will be mind-blowing; we'll just pass out and get up speechless, unable to believe our eyes. When we gaze upon God, all we'll be able to do is cry, "Holy! Holy! Holy! Lord God Almighty."

Do you know that there will be no need of light there, because God will be our eternal light? We'll no longer be servants, but kings and queens, and we'll be served by angels. When the angels approach us, they will hide their faces and say, "Holy! Holy! Holy!" Why? Who are we? It has not yet been revealed what we will be, but we will be like Him. Do you know that believers are the bride of Christ? There will be no sickness, no pain, no sadness, no sorrow, and absolutely no form of sin in Heaven. The old things will all pass away, and behold, all things will become new. That day is soon approaching, so we need to do the work of Him who called us before it's too late.

If we could view the supernatural from Earth, we'd realize how microscopic we are. We're the size of bacteria compared to a little segment of Heaven. With this pinhole view, we're able to capture mysteries untold; astonishingly, we'd see our future displayed like a work of art waiting to manifest in the natural. The supernatural is beyond our imagination, beyond our wildest dreams. We'd have the ability to fly anywhere within that realm, disappearing and reappearing anywhere. It's impossible for anything to die there, because everything is supernatural. The flowers never die, and food never stops growing.

Think about Hell and Heaven for a moment... one spiritual realm, yet two very different places. Everything in Hell lasts for eternity—never to die, never to cease. In Hell, everything is opposite to Heaven. There is pain, sickness, sorrow, and deterioration, whereas in Heaven, you'll find joy, love, happiness, goodness, and good health. The supernatural is beyond our limits, so we can't comprehend it with the finite mind. Many believe that the supernatural is a fairy tale just because they can't understand it. The same could be said about foreign languages. They are worse than a fairy tale to me. Some languages sound as though people are speaking gibberish, which sounds like nonsense to me, yet they are real languages that can be understood by others. Another person's opinion doesn't change the facts; what might appear as nonsense or a fairy tale could possibly be a reality.

5. OUR PROTECTION FROM THE ENEMY

OUR FUTURE ETERNAL DESTINY IS NOT THE ONLY PART OF LIFE THAT IS wrapped up in Christ. Many of the situations that we presently face have their solutions in Christ through the Word. People everywhere are in despair because of the natural effect on the Earth of the fall of man in Genesis. The forces of darkness are working hard. Principalities and powers and rulers of darkness in high places have set up their camp everywhere and are fighting against us. If one is in Christ, he is protected from all harm: *"The angel of the LORD encampeth round about them that fear him, and delivereth them,"* (Psalm 34:7).

Psalm 91:1-6 says:

> *He that dwelleth in the secret place of the most High shall abide under the shadow of the Almighty. I will say of the LORD, He is my refuge and my fortress: my God; in him will I trust. Surely he shall deliver thee from the snare of the fowler, and from the noisome pestilence. He shall cover thee with his feathers, and under his wings shalt thou trust: his truth shall be thy shield and buckler. Thou shalt not be afraid for the terror by night; nor for the arrow that flieth by day; Nor for the pestilence that walketh in darkness; nor for the destruction that wasteth at noonday.*

All believers are protected from the enemy and therefore do not need to be afraid. God has supernaturally covered us with an invisible shield. His angels are fighting and protecting us at all times. Because of the supernatural laws that are in place, we can be targets to the enemy if we're not in line with the spiritual laws. This is why God warns us in His Word to put on the whole armour so that we'll be protected at all times. We can only be unprotected if we refuse to wear our protection.

6. LAWS IN THE SPIRITUAL THAT DICTATE THE NATURAL

God is the Centre of the Spiritual/Supernatural

THE SAME LAW OR PRINCIPLES THAT GOVERN BOTH THE NATURAL AND THE spiritual world caused the world to come into being. This law has nothing to do with religion. It supernaturally existed before creation. Whether or not we believe in a god, we are all connected to a spiritual being. Call it what you want— Mother Nature, karma, or science—it's still God. God has established these laws to regulate the world, and no one can change them. Some of the laws in the natural have become such a part of our everyday lives that we don't even consider them laws. Christians and non-Christians abide by these laws.

Spiritual laws work just the same as natural laws—you have to follow the law whether you like it or not. Some of us are perishing because we aren't following the spiritual law. Let's take a look at a natural law like gravity. Jump off a cliff, and sooner or later you'll find out if it works. If you understand how the natural law works, you can understand how the spiritual law works. Natural laws, such as rules and regulations, are governed, regulated, and enforced by the law, and they are compulsory. You're required to follow certain laws, and if you don't, there will be consequences.

Let's take a look at everyday principles. If you don't seek after things in the natural, you might not obtain them. Certain goals will never be achieved if we don't take action; however, the spiritual realm dictates what happens in the natural realm. For certain things to happen in the natural, we have to call it forth from the spiritual. The creation of the world is a good example. In Genesis 1, we're told that the heavens and the natural world came into being by God calling them forth. God spoke and said "*let there be light,*" and there was light (Genesis 1:3). He obeys His own law. I am telling you that there is a mystery in the law of the spiritual. God is all powerful. He could have created this world without any decree or laws, but He did chose not to.

The words that we speak have power; therefore, we must be careful how we use them. On the spiritual level, we need to call things into being before they can happen. Let me ask you a question: Can a person go to jail if the judge doesn't speak the sentence into being? No. A murderer can sit in the conviction chair forever and not go behind bars unless the judge decrees it so. Likewise, a man cannot be freed from jail unless the parole board, a legal authority, decrees it so. Guilty or not guilty, it takes words to confirm the conviction so that the truth can come into operation.

As the royal priesthood through Christ, we are blessed beyond measure; however, all of our blessings will just sit there until eternity if we don't claim them. The spiritual law also requires that we take our case before the supernatural judge and claim our rights through prayer before He will release them unto us. Not only is the spiritual waiting for us to decree things, but when we speak, we are prophesying. Do you realize that the experiences of many people are a result of what they decree into their lives or allow someone else to decree? Some people are always negative; all they speak is doom. As a result, their lives are exactly what they speak— doom. Could all these negative things be coming from Hell? I believe so, because all bad things come from the enemy. We have the power to decree things from the spiritual, whether good or bad.

Even Satan works according to the laws of the supernatural. Not only must he abide by certain laws, but he also loves to release the destruction contained in those laws to bring about our downfall. He will feed our thoughts with counterfeit things like sickness, poverty, or even someone else's husband. Satan feeds this garbage into us because we allow it, but it's not what God originally intended. We were created to inherit the real stuff. We are told in the Word that if we decree something, it shall come to pass. It doesn't matter what it looks like in the natural; we must prophesy what it looks like in the spiritual. Send the word, decree something that is already in the spiritual, and it will come to pass. If you're poor, don't keep saying that you're poor; instead, decree that you are rich, and it will come to pass sooner or later. There is life and death in the power of the tongue. With our words we can open up all supernatural opportunities and blessings by just calling them into being. Prophesy them into being. Jesus walked with this authority and expects us to follow. Jesus spoke to the wind and storms and they obeyed Him. Some storms and winds in our lives will not leave unless we speak to them.

Even the Unsaved Are Governed by Certain Laws

I conducted some research among people who don't have a relationship with God and discovered that they practice certain principles that produce benefits, particularly in the area of giving. There is a law of giving and receiving. Give and it shall be given back unto you; everything in the universe operates through exchange. Even God operates through that law. God sent his only son in exchange for man's redemption.

There is also a law concerning giving a portion of one's income as a tithe. Many people practice this. Jews, Muslims, and Hindus are very successful because of this law. Why is this? I believe that the laws of the supernatural are already established and apply to everyone. Do good, and good will come back to you. Some called it karma, but I call it established law. Whatever seed one sows, one will reap. This fact is often taken for granted. Many people are suffering as a result of the bad seeds they sow; ironically, the unsaved are functioning in the law of the spiritual and benefiting from it. All human being have a spiritual side and can function in the supernatural. The Scripture says that the Lord rains on the just and on the unjust (Matthew 5:45).

If the unsaved receive benefits from the supernatural, how much more will the Christians who are connected to the supernatural God? We need to come out of our negative beliefs and develop a positive outlook on life. Some generational curses that have followed families throughout the years are of a spiritual nature and need to be broken.

You must reject those curses and start speaking positive things into your life. If you're in poverty, decree that you are rich; if you're sick, decree that you are healthy. If you're living a defeated life, please try this principle and watch it work. I'm not telling you to try something that I've never tried. For years I was living a defeated life, unable to understand this principle. I constantly decreed negative things over my life and watched them come to pass. I never understood this principle until people from all walks of life started to call me the voodoo woman.

During that time, whenever someone would do something wrong against me, I would decree something bad towards then. Believe me, whatever I spoke would happen within days. I then realized that I have the power to speak things into being, so I stopped speaking bad things and started to speak good things. My life has changed as a result of decreeing positive things. I no longer accept what things look like, but look towards what will happen in due time.

Using Faith with the Law of God

Speak the word and watch it come to pass. I don't know if I used faith. All I knew was that I spoke and things happened; however, faith is a great agent that causes the supernatural to intervene on our behalf. In the book of Matthew, the Lord says that if we have faith as a mustard seed, and we ask believing we will receive, it will be done (17:20). Many things are available to us, but we must believe when we ask. We'll stay stagnant in life if we don't take action in the natural to gain access to the supernatural realm. The Bible says that faith without works is dead (James 2:20); therefore, if we sit by while waiting for things to happen in our lives and don't act, we will achieve nothing. The Bible says, "... *seek, and ye shall find; knock, and it shall be opened ...*" (Matthew 7:7).

The Law of the Word of God

His Word is spiritual and true. God's Word cannot be stopped, altered, broken, or cancelled. It was designed to accomplish what it sets out to be and do. The Word is God, and God cannot lie. For the Word to work in your situation, you must have faith.

Spiritual Hospital Manual

There are so many things we think we need in life, but they are hindrances that block the flow of the supernatural God's power in our lives.

- Because God is love, He does everything through love. In order for supernatural blessings to flow in an individual's life, they must have love. The lack of love hinders the work of God.
- God's law also requires us to forgive; therefore; if we desire God to intervene on our behalf, we must first forgive. God will not perform a miracle in our life if we are walking in unforgiveness.
- Unbelief will block supernatural release in your life. The Bible says that if you have faith as small as a mustard seed ...
- Demonic spirits lie behind many of the hindrances in our lives, so they must be dealt with in order to obtain release. God's law requires decree. Decree what God has instructed us to do in His Word to produce results. We have the power to bind the strong man (Matthew 12:28, 29). Use the Word of God and the name of Jesus to bind up any demonic blockage.

7. SPIRITUAL WARFARE: SECRETS OF THE ENEMY!

I'M GOING TO EXPOSE THE ENEMY IN THIS BOOK SO THAT YOU'LL HAVE A GOOD understanding of how he works, and then you can counter-attack him. Let's call this study "Spiritual Bacteria and Infection" (Satan, demons, evil spirits). The Body of Christ is living in defeat and perishing because of lack of knowledge. The enemy doesn't want people to know who he really is, or that he's the source behind most of their problems. It's not even worth going through the immeasurable blessings God has for His people, because some people won't even believe it, never mind walk in them. This is the strategy of the enemy!

Let's recognize that God is omnipresent and can be in all places at the same time. Satan is very limited and can only be in one place at a time. He uses his demons to inform him. Most of the time we're fighting one of his demons. The more of a threat we are to him, or the closer we are to God, the more he'll pursue us. He'll even use a stronger demon to fight us. He himself will pursue us if his demons are not at the level to manage us.

Satan Has Limited Power

God is the only true source of power. When Satan was kicked out of Heaven, he was stripped of his power. Most people believe that the devil is powerful, but that is one of Satan's biggest tricks. He magnifies himself to make people think he is powerful, but to a Christian, he's just a little ant who's afraid of us. Satan has often met with success because Christians sit back in their comfort zones doing nothing while watching Satan fight. It's time the Body of Christ got up and started to do something about all the havoc Satan and his demon are creating. If we were to fight back, there wouldn't be so many problems in the world. Christians are more powerful than the enemy. We have the sovereign God's limitless power at our disposal.

Satan's power lies in our weakness or in what we give him. Whenever we fulfill the lusts of the flesh, we're feeding the devil with power. If we stopped doing evil and obeyed God, then Satan wouldn't have any power over us. Satan usually provokes our weak points and patiently waits for us to fall prey. His power is fake; he can't work a real miracle. He attempts to convince us of his twisted lies, which aim to destroy, hamper, or prevent our sense of identity and purpose in Christ. If we destroy his many delusions, then he has no power over us.

Satan has different ranks of demons that are well organized and very loyal to him. They faithfully carry out his tasks for him. I wondered why these demons are so faithful to Satan, and it came to me that Satan doesn't allow free will. God's ultimate love allows humans to make free choices, but Satan is void of love and cannot allow free will.

Satan will whisper in your ear that all the promises of the Bible are a lie, including the cross and the blood of Jesus. You might not understand the different voices in your ears, so you feed the lies until they become programmed into your conscious mind. You then retrieve all the other bad things that you've learned and experienced that were previously stored in your subconscious mind. Finally, you process that information, believing the lies of the enemy. The lies now begin to grow and affect the way you live your life.

Satan's Organized Board

Principalities—This includes the chief ruler, the head, Satan's chair of authority, the Prince of Darkness, prince of this world. All the evil in the world comes by his authority.

Powers—These are the demons that work alongside Satan to carry out missions to control countries, territories, and towns. They cause corruption, havoc, and disorder for the governments, heads of nations, heads of organizations, and heads of churches through greed, perversion, lust, and wars.

Ruler of Darkness—These demons keep people divided by undercover darkness. They stop the coherence of peace, kindness, and trust among mankind. They plan confusion, hate, jealousy, and conflict among people.

Spiritual Wickedness—These are the wicked spirits in the heavens. They don't want to see people give true and sincere worship to God, so they work hard to control it. They can also control all forms of authority, the legal system, MPs, mayors, presidents, and prime ministers. New age adherents, cults, psychics, and voodoo workers are all under the control of spiritual wickedness.

High Places—These are areas of information that the demons desire to control, such as TV, radio, newspapers, and church pulpits.

Scripture references—Colossians 1:16-18, 2:10; Ephesians 1:21, 2:2, 6:12; John 14:30, 16:11.

Satan is outnumbered. Only one third of the angels fell with the devil. That means two-thirds of the angels, along with Christians, are fighting on God's behalf. Satan can't confront all believers around the globe at the same time. Even when he does attack, it's with limited resources. The devil is always outnumbered and completely overpowered. We can stand and resist him, and he will flee!

Scripture Reference to the Secret of Satan

Satan's Kingdom cannot hold us. Colossians 1:13 tells us that we have been delivered from the power of darkness into a marvellous light and into the kingdom of Heaven of God. We can sit in heavenly places with Christ, even while we are here on Earth.

Satan Does Not Own Anything Legally (He Is Using Stolen Authority)

> *For by him were all things created, that are in heaven, and that are in earth, visible and invisible, whether they be thrones, or*

> dominions, or principalities, or powers: all things were created by him, and for him.
>
> —Colossians 1:16

The devil needs our permission and God's permission to do anything to us, but because the enemy is very deceptive, he determines our level of willpower and utilizes it to his disposal.

Satan Can Be Controlled by Us

> And the seventy returned again with joy, saying, Lord, even the devils are subject unto us through thy name. Behold, I give unto you power to tread on serpents and scorpions, and over all the power of the enemy: and nothing shall by any means hurt you.
>
> —Luke 10:17,19

Satan Is Limited in Temptations

> There hath no temptation taken you but such as is common to man: but God is faithful, who will not suffer you to be tempted above that ye are able; but will with the temptation also make a way to escape, that ye may be able to bear it.
>
> —1 Corinthians 10:13

Satan Wants to Keep the World in Darkness

> But if our gospel be hid, it is hid to them that are lost: In whom the god of this world hath blinded the minds of them which believe not, lest the light of the glorious gospel of Christ, who is the image of God, should shine unto them.
>
> —2 Corinthians 4:3-4

The Devil Is a Created Being Like Us

Satan is completely locked out of the knowledge of the mind of God. He can't read our minds, but he will study us and try to develop different tactics to get us to do his work. As children of God filled with the Holy Spirit, we can come to understand and know the heart and mind of God.

Satan cannot create anything; instead, he manipulates what God created. For example, Satan fills music with all kinds of spirits to lure people into sin, even though music itself is good. Sex is good. God made it a pleasurable thing for marriage and child bearing, but Satan uses it to cause destruction, twisted relationships, disease, and perversion. A good way to describe Satan's tricks is to compare them to a pie. He bakes a beautiful pie that smells good, tastes good, and looks delicious, but he'll mix it full of poo (evil).

Jesus has stripped Satan of his key weapons. "*And having disarmed the powers and authorities, he made a public spectacle of them, triumphing over them by the cross,*" (Colossians 2:15, NIV). If we accept Jesus as our Lord and Saviour, we'll have life forever. Satan has nothing new; he uses the same tricks over and over. His strategy is to attack us with the same habitual temptations in our lives.

> *For all that is in the world, the lust of the flesh, and the lust of the eyes, and the pride of life, is not of the Father, but is of the world. And the world passeth away, and the lust thereof: but he that doeth the will of God abideth for ever.*
>
> —I John 2:16-17

Knowing all of this, why is the enemy winning over the children of God? The enemy is very crafty. He knows your openings, weaknesses, and vulnerabilities. He understands your tendencies. He's like a snake under grass, plotting for you to trip, fall, and eventually fail. You won't be able to identify him standing before you as a monster, a ghost, a wolf, or a demon in a red suit with horns and a tail and blowing fire from his mouth. He's much subtler. He is disguised, camouflaged. Like a wolf in sheep's clothing.

Deborah Nembhard-Colquhoun

Spiritual Warfare

A Definition of Spiritual Warfare

Spiritual warfare refers to a war that is taking place in the unseen realm, the spiritual realm, that is affecting us in the natural realm. The two realms are intertwined; because the spiritual realm is so close, it lies within our very hearts.

Spiritual warfare is the universal war of good versus evil. It is a daily battle between God and Satan; between the Christian, the Church, and the world system ruled by our spiritual enemy; and within every child of God, between the Holy Spirit and the lusts of the flesh.

In Ephesians 6:12, Paul writes: *"For we wrestle not against flesh and blood, but against principalities, against powers, against the rulers of the darkness of this world, against spiritual wickedness in high places."* You don't wrestle against the person who lied to you, opposed you, hurt you, or blocked your way at work or church, but against the different ranks of evil power in the demonic kingdom.

Unfortunately, Satan is invisible, and he is 100 per cent pure evil. No matter what you do, you can never please this enemy. You can't make a deal, you can't negotiate or bargain, and you can't argue logically. He is permanently evil. The Bible says he is like a roaring lion seeking whom he may devour. He comes to kill, steal, and destroy (1 Peter 5:8). Satan doesn't want you... he hates you. He's just using you because he needs a body in which to operate. As Satan is a spiritual being, he is operating illegally in the earthly realm. Humans were the only ones given authority to operate and have dominion in the earthly realm, so anyone or anything that is not human is operating without our or God's permission. Fortunately, the power we have at our disposal is more powerful than him.

Why Is the Enemy Fighting?

Satan is mad at God, so he's battling to destroy the thing that God loves so much—mankind. His goal is to destroy the image of God and to strip mankind of their power and authority by deception and manipulation. He's also jealous of mankind, because we have the hope of eternity. Everything that God has given and blessed us with in our lives, Satan battles to take away. After death, he wants nothing to do with us. He's only after our life, our soul, our destiny, our future, our eternal destiny, and the breath of God that dwells inside of us. He knows the blessed hope you have in Jesus, and he's going to try everything in his power to block and destroy you.

Satan and his evil spirits desire to keep us ignorant, bound, and out of the Kingdom of God. The Kingdom of God is the will of God in our lives, and God's rule and reign. Anything outside the Kingdom of God is living and walking in the flesh. Being in the flesh, we are often under Satan's control.

Where Does Satan Attack Us?

Pretty much everywhere, as long as it will impact man and his belief in God.

Your Mind

Spiritual warfare takes place in the mind of every believer. In our minds, we wrestle and struggle against the lusts of the flesh, the lusts of the eyes, the pride of life, and the devil— worldly desire and principles that will lure us into sin. Our mind is the hard drive for our entire body; it contains our thoughts (imagination, reasoning, and intellect), and it holds our emotions and will. It's by our thoughts and feelings that we determine our will and purpose for our life; therefore, if our minds are affected, our entire lives are affected. This is why the mind is the enemy's main target.

Your Body

Satan will attack you with sicknesses and diseases.

Your Relationships

Satan attacks the things and people that are close and valuable to you—relationships, family, marriages, businesses, finances, and other valuables.

Deborah Nembhard-Colquhoun

How Do You Know When You Are under a Spiritual Attack?

One of the main signs of a spiritual attack is the loss of desire for spiritual things. You lose your desire to read the Word, pray, and serve God passionately. You feel exhausted; your strength is diminished, you're physically drained, you lack of focus, and you feel overwhelmed or paralyzed. There is havoc and confusion in the church and in your household.

Spiritual attacks also occur when Christians or churches fight amongst themselves, or when you're doing something in the church out of obligation and not desire. All the resources around you dry up, including your finances. Your vehicle breaks down, your wife or husband leaves you, your children give you trouble, your business deteriorates, and everything seems to go wrong at the same time. You feel depressed, perplexed, and in some cases when you're sick or feeling guilty, you feel helpless and hopeless. It's prayer time, but the phone starts to ring or you suddenly feel sleepy.

A married couple can come under attack when one person can't seem to resist the feelings they have towards someone else and may feel like cheating. You can come under attack when you'd do anything to get another person's position. You've been redeemed by the power of God, and He has cast all your sins into the sea of forgetfulness, but you still feel condemned by your past. Guilt is choking. You have been lied to. And the list goes on and on ...

What are some secrets to victory in spiritual warfare, and what are your defence weapons?

The Whole Armour

To put on the whole armour, you must first have a strong relationship with God. We draw our spiritual strength from God, which requires us to be fully dependent on and obedient to Him. Wearing the full armour protects every part of you from the fiery darts of the enemy. Your armour consists of the following parts: truth, righteousness, readiness to share the Gospel, faith, salvation, the Word of God, and prayer. Spiritual warfare maintains your healing, your deliverance, your peace, and your prosperity; this is the victory that God has given to all believers.

How Do You Fight When the Enemy Comes at You?

Overcome evil with good. Resist the enemy by doing something good in a bad situation. Be at peace with the people that bring harm to you by forgiving them of their wrongdoings. Saturate yourself in the Holy Spirit, because Satan is afraid of the Spirit and cannot come near you when you are in the Spirit.

Giving is a form of spiritual warfare. When you give, God destroys the devourer and He opens up the heavens and pours out blessings upon you.

The Word of God is a powerful weapon. Follow the example of Jesus when the enemy comes to you with deceptions and use the Word against him. Pray in the Spirit. Our defense is Jesus Christ, who is interceding on our behalf. We need to turn to Him by faith, and He will fight our battles. Make praise and worship a daily exercise. Praise brings forth God's presence, which the enemy hates and will flee from. When you are overtaken with pride, conquer the enemy by surrendering to God.

How to Identify When You Are under the Control of the Enemy

You know the enemy is controlling you if you're operating in contradiction to the will of God, especially if you're yielding to the lust of the flesh, which produces pride, idolatry, witchcraft, hatred, fornication, adultery, uncleanness, lasciviousness, wrath, gossip, strife, sedition, envy, drunkenness, and murder. All of this can be found in Scripture.

8. WHY IS THERE A NEED FOR A SPIRITUAL HOSPITAL?

MOST SICKNESSES ARE SPIRITUAL AND CANNOT BE HEALED WITH MEDICAL intervention alone. Spiritual Hospital targets the spiritual issues and deals with them in supernatural ways that the medical system cannot handle. Let's face it—we live in a fallen world. Spiritual Hospital is here to come alongside those who are sick physically, emotionally, sociologically, and psychologically.

Let's look at the original cause of sickness. God created mankind to be perfect and to possess authority, wealth, and perfect health. We were to enjoy life to its fullest, but as Christians know well, there was a major spiritual attack at the beginning of creation. Mankind disobeyed God, yielded to Satan's tricks, and became contaminated with the nasty, destructive sin disease. As a result, we lost favour with God ... and our perfect health. Not only does Spiritual Hospital provide help beyond what medicine and science can offer, but we help to prepare people for the security of their eternal home.

Sicknesses in countless forms resulted from Adam and Eve's original sin. Humankind is now subject to disease, illness, and deterioration. Many of the unfortunate issues faced by man today are the result of this devastation. The natural hospital is there to aid with the physical part of this devastation, but the spiritual aspect also needs to be dealt with, and this is how the Spiritual Hospital can help.

Not only are we susceptible to disease, but without an intervention, we became spiritually dead and will eventually die. Romans 5:12 states, "*Wherefore, as by one man sin entered into the world, and death by sin; and so death passed upon all men, for that all have sinned ..."* Mankind does not have the ability or the desire to overcome sin or bring himself from the state of spiritual death back to life. One might ask: "Why do I need to be alive spiritually when I am functioning physically?" Although mankind has a physical side, the more important part is the spiritual. Whether we want to believe it or not, there is a good and a bad supernatural eternity, and where we go after death will depend upon our spiritual condition. Understand that one must be born again spiritually to be able to go to the good side of the supernatural.

> *Jesus answered, Verily, verily, I say unto thee, Except a man be born of water and of the Spirit, he cannot enter into the kingdom of God. That which is born of the flesh is flesh; and that which is born of the Spirit is spirit.*
>
> —John 3:5-6

Just as we can't give physical birth to ourselves, we can't accomplish this spiritual birth by ourselves, either. God gives it, but through faith in Christ we must request it.

We Are Commissioned to Share the Gospel

Christians are expected to evangelize. It's not an option, but a command. God gave us the Gospel to share. Christ commands all Christians in Matthew 28:19-20 to share the Good News:

> *Go ye therefore, and teach all nations, baptizing them in the name of the Father, and of the Son, and of the Holy Ghost: Teaching them to observe all things whatsoever I have commanded you: and, lo, I am with you always, even unto the end of the world. Amen.*

Have you ever wondered why God doesn't take us to Heaven immediately after we're saved? I've thought about this, and I believe that Christ is still preparing a place for mankind. Ultimately, we're here on Earth for one reason—to preach the Gospel. God can speed up His construction in Heaven any time, but He chooses not to because He has imprinted upon mankind His plan to use us as His vessels to bring redemption to the world.

Paul writes in 1 Corinthians 9:16-23:

> *For though I preach the gospel, I have nothing to glory of: for necessity is laid upon me; yea, woe is unto me, if I preach not the gospel! For if I do this thing willingly, I have a reward: but if against my will, a dispensation of the gospel is committed unto me. What is my reward then? Verily that, when I preach the gospel, I may make the gospel of Christ without charge, that I abuse not my power in the gospel. For though I be free from all men, yet have I made myself servant unto all, that I might gain the more. And unto the Jews I became as a Jew, that I might gain the Jews; to them that are under the law, as under the law, that I might gain them that are under the law; To them that are without law, as without law, (being not without law to God, but under the law to Christ,) that I might gain them that are without law. To the weak became I as weak, that I might gain the weak: I am made all things to all men that I might by all means save some. And this I do for the gospel's sake, that I might be partaker thereof with you.*

"Preaching the Gospel," according to Dr. Rondo Thomas, Vice President of Canada Christian College, "is not only by words, but also by lifestyle." Our lives are open books that the unsaved may read. What are they to read when they look at us and the lives we lead? They should see Christ in us and all over us; they should read the story of Christ-like character in us. What would Christ do? We are to exhibit the same character as Christ. In this way, people may read the living words in the Bible as they are being applied to our lives. For example, our lives can show the fruits of the Spirit, which are love, joy, peace, longsuffering, gentleness, goodness, faith, meekness, and temperance (Galatians 5:22-23). It's impossible for the sovereign Christ to be alive in us and for His presence to go unnoticed.

Deborah Nembhard-Colquhoun

There Is a Great Harvest of Souls (Spiritual Dead) in the World to Reap

"*The harvest truly is plenteous, but the labourers are few; Pray ye therefore the Lord of the harvest, that he will send forth labourers into his harvest,*" (Matthew 9:37-38). The world is the field in which the ready harvest is available, the Word is the seed in the hearts of the unsaved (the ready harvest), and the workers are the Christians.

God has used some to plant seeds and some to water. He has convicted the hearts of the lost, and is now looking for those who are available to reap the ready harvest. Are you a ready vessel, available to be used for Christ in winning souls? If you are, all you need to do is take up your baskets, go to the field, and allow God to fill them with souls.

How Will They Believe Unless They Have Heard?

> *How then shall they call on him in whom they have not believed? And how shall they believe in him of whom they have not heard? And how shall they hear without a preacher? And how shall they preach, except they be sent? As it is written, how beautiful are the feet of them that preach the gospel of peace, and bring glad tidings of good things! But they have not all obeyed the gospel. For Esaias saith, Lord, who hath believed our report? So then faith cometh by hearing, and hearing by the word of God.*
>
> —Romans 10:14-17

The ultimate purpose of Spiritual Hospital is to deliver people from the spiritual inherited sin disease.

9. THE SUPERNATURAL GOD WANTS US HEALED

MANY PEOPLE HAVE EMBRACED ILLNESS, NOT UNDERSTANDING THAT IT'S NOT God's will for them to be sick. Not only was it God's original plan for us to live in good health, but He left His spiritual splendour (Heaven) so that we could be in good health again.

We live in a deprived world where sickness is real and everyone will eventually face an illness. Some are quickly healed, others take longer, and others are never healed. Even though the Bible explains the origins of sickness, many people are still confused, especially the unbelievers. Some people blame sickness on viruses, bacteria, and genetics. Society believes that if we could get rid of all diseases, we would be fine. This is why medical associations try to find new drugs to heal diseases. Others blame illness on genetics or the environment. They believe that if we preserve the Earth, we can be healed. Some even go so far as to blame aliens from outer space! Even God is blamed for all the sicknesses.

Sickness is not only physical, but it can be mental, emotional, physiological, and spiritual. We're living in a sick world ... a deprived world. The Lord God says:

> *If my people, which are called by my name, shall humble themselves, and pray, and seek my face, and turn from their wicked ways; then will I hear from heaven, and will forgive their sin, and will heal their land.*
>
> —2 Chronicles 7:14

The world is not too sick to be healed by God. The churches are also sick. You might be physically sound but suffer from a broken heart or a broken relationship. Financial lack is a form of sickness, too.

Ezekiel saw the dry bones in the valley; they had no flesh or marrow, but they were able to come back to life. This vision was of Israel being restored. We are spiritual Israel, and we too can be healed. We can be restored from all our sickness and from all that the caterpillar has eaten away and the conger worm has destroyed.

God originally made man free from every sickness. We were made in God's image, and God has no trace of sickness in Him; therefore, we originally were sickness-free. Genesis 1:31 states that *"God saw all that he had made, and it was very good,"* (NIV). Notice the words *"very good."* Not just good, but very good— no blemish, free from every trace of imperfection, just as God is holy with no trace of imperfection. We are made in His image. Some people exaggerate and call things good when they're not, but God is not a God who lies. He only gives good gifts, and sickness is far from being good! *"Every good gift and every perfect gift is from above, and cometh down from the Father of lights, with whom is no variableness, neither shadow of turning,"* (James 1:17).

The thief wants us sick. The devil is a thief who *"... cometh not, but for to steal, and to kill, and to destroy ..."* (John 10:10a). Sickness does the same thing to us. It steals our health and destroys our lives prematurely. God, on the other hand, declares *"I am come that they might have life, and that they might have it more abundantly,"* (John 10:10b). The first thing God gave man was His image. Don't you think God did this because He wanted mankind to look like Him, act like Him, and live like Him? Looking, living, and acting like Him is not to be in sickness. The second thing God did was to place man in His presence, which in the Hebrew language represents Eden. Man not only has the opportunity to enjoy all these privileges, but to be in God's presence, the garden of delight.

Although we are human, we are also spiritual beings living in a physical experience. The real you and me is trapped in a house we call the body. The ideal environment that God intended for us to be in is in His presence at all times. Anything that is designed to be in a certain environment but is not will malfunction. Just like a fish out of water.

Many people blame their sickness on different sources. Satan is the root source, but my Bible tells me that man brought sin on himself. Even though we didn't sin in the garden, a little part of Adam lives in us. We inherited the sin nature passed down from Adam. Through one man, sin enters the world. It was because of disobedience that we're faced with sickness today. God specifically told Adam and Eve not to eat of the tree of the knowledge of good and evil, but they refused to listen. We see examples of this throughout Scripture. God told Israel that if they touched fire, they would get burned. Satan tempted Jesus. Not everything that looks good to the eye is good for us.

Biblical Diagnosis Versus Spiritual Diagnosis

The biblical diagnosis of our fallen human condition is sin. Before there was any sin in the world, everything was perfect. There were no sicknesses or diseases, neither physical nor emotional; therefore, we can diagnose all emotional sickness as being caused by sin.

The biblical intervention for this sickness is confession (James 5:16; 1 John 1:9) and repentance, which is a resolute turning away from sin. This includes baptism into the death of Jesus Christ (Romans 6:3), crucifixion with Christ (Galatians 2:20), and death to self (Colossians 3:3).

10. HOW WE CONDUCT PROCEDURES FOR SPIRITUAL SICKNESS

We have a tendency to focus our attention on other people for our spiritual healing. Pastors, evangelists, and bishops are only vessels that God uses to perform His work. Our eyes must be set on Jesus, who is the ultimate healer. We are all nothing without God.

Standard procedure:

Spiritual healing requires a spiritual diagnosis, which we define as the identification of the root causes of the disease or condition from its symptoms.

- The initial examination is done with spiritual radar, spiritual laser, or spiritual X-Ray specialists. We interpret these as individuals whom God has equipped with different spiritual gifts—you know them as prophets, discerners, and intercessors. They conduct the initial examination by looking deep into the spiritual side of a person and identifying the disease.
- These tests are often done while individuals are being prayed for one on one. Tests are sometimes done randomly. As a person enters the doors or while in the service, they can be spotted by one of our spiritual specialists. In addition, even without the person being present, the specialist can see their conditions.

Spiritual Interventions
Spiritual Operation, Spiritual Medication, Spiritual Therapy, Spiritual Nutrition

Preparation before operation:

- Diagnosis is made after the spiritual examination, and then a confession can be declared, acknowledging the cause of the spiritual sickness. Spiritual maintenance (cleansing and disinfection) is administrated. The individual must search himself and forgive anyone against whom they hold unforgiveness. They must turn away completely from their old sinful ways with a humble and contrite heart. In addition, the individual must be in compliance with all the commandments of God.

The initial operation:

- Dr. Jesus has already conducted the operation in the spirit at Calvary over 2000 years ago, but it needs to be carried out in the natural through his vessels (ministers). Dr. Jesus taught His disciples how to perform healings and cast out demons, telling them that they have power and authority and that they would do greater works through the Holy Spirit. Today we are just as qualified as any bishop, Christian doctor, or pastor to perform healings. He also left His spiritual instruction manual for us to refer to daily. Did you know that most doctors refer to their medical manual daily?
- After we conduct the examination and find the problem, we use the injection needle (our mouth) that contains the medication (the Word of God). Again, we use the double edged sword (the Word of God) and faith (to turn the trigger) with force (authority) to destroy every spiritual infirmity.

- To heal the affected area, we use another instrument of the Word of God. Understand that the Word of God is a multipurpose tool.
- Please note that when a wound is cut, it will feel sore. It might still hurt or even hurt more, so it must be treated properly. If not treated properly, the infection might return (spirits, demons).
- The surgery area (deliverance) need to be bathed in prayer, anointed with praise and worship, medicated with the Word, and bandaged with the belt of truth three times a day. In addition to this directive and depending on the condition, a checkup may be needed once a week until complete healing has occurred. In case of emergency, you are to call the twenty-four-hour line or come in to the next scheduled service.

Please do not try this procedure yourself:

- If you are a new Christian (training is needed as there can be major repercussions)
- If you are unsaved
- If you are a Christian and living in sin. You can't be living and sleeping with the devil and expect to cast him out: "*Jesus I know, and Paul I know, but who are you?*" (Act 19:15).

You and I can perform signs and wonders, but we fall short because we're lacking in knowledge. No one can do it like Jesus ... He will leave no stone unturned.

For my thoughts are not your thoughts, neither are your ways my ways, saith the LORD. For as the heavens are higher than the earth, so are my ways higher than your ways, and my thoughts than your thoughts.

—Isaiah 55:8–9

As the Holy Spirit sees fit procedure:

We call this "the glory realm" procedure. The glory realm is the atmosphere of God, or the manifestation of God Himself as the only true and living God. When God's glory comes down, it's a bit of Heaven's environment coming down to us. In this glory realm, anything is possible. Signs and wonders will manifest right before our eyes. The blind will see, limbs will grow back, cancer will disappear, and the lame will walk. All of our needs can be met, because He is in our midst.

Once the room is set up properly, God through His Holy Spirit will conduct all necessary healings and deliverance. The only help that might be required is the help of the nurse (angels of the Lord). In this realm, you will hear people crying out, "I am healed; I am healed," even though no one laid a hand on them. God alone gets the glory with this procedure.

Before this procedure can take place, the room and the authorities must be attended to. For example, ushers, pastors, ministers, and altar workers must be disinfected and sterilized from all spiritual bacteria (pride, self-glory, gossip, hate, backbiting, sexual immorality, witchcraft). The instruments (worshippers, preachers, musicians) must receive special attention. Believers are required to live in obedience to God, and this obedience starts with the authority that God put in place in His church. The authority figures are there not to contaminate the Body of Christ, but to lead others into right standing. God works within the boundaries of certain laws, and if there is a hindrance, it will block Him from working. God is holy and will not mix with uncleanness in His church.

You might think that your church is doing fine, but could it be that it's operating with strange fire? It might have a form of godliness, but no manifestation of God's power. It's sad to say, but there is hardly any healing and deliverance taking place in most churches today. God wants to move like never before, but He's waiting on the church to clean up the filth so He can come in and perform miracles, signs, and wonders.

There's a difference between having a spiritual disease for which the root cause is sin, and living in sin or presumptuous sin. It's possible for the glory realm to be amongst us, but for a person to be unaware of it because of the heavy sin in which they are involved. This is why many people attend church and receive their blessing, while some go back the same way they came. Let's examine how the glory realm comes into our midst and how an individual can enter the glory realm.

Four Keys to Enter This Realm

- Faith: There are many ways to enter into the supernatural realm, but only through faith in Jesus Christ can one enter into the glory realm.
- Holiness and humility: Without holiness, no one will see God (Hebrews 12:14).
- Praise and Worship: It is of foremost importance that worship is clean and sanitized from all sin bacteria, because praise is the main activity that consecrates the presence of the Lord in our midst. Praise changes the atmosphere, and true worship sustains that realm. Praise and worship are two important keys that unlock the route into the glory realm. The psalmist said to enter into His presence with praise. He dwells within our praise. God inhabits the praises of His people. He dwells in our very presence.

As we press deeper in our praise and worship with God, the spiritual capacity of God's presence increases to an amazing climax. From that level, we move from the Presence Realm to the Glory Realm, where your spiritual sensitivity is at its highest. Your spiritual eyes are bright; your spiritual hearing is alert. This is where your faith is strong and your gifting is alive.

The spiritual side of true worship is warfare. This is the only place Satan can't touch you. This kind of worship stops Satan in his tracks. The supernatural is accessible; miracles, signs, and wonders take place. In this realm, demons will flee, chains will be broken, and yokes destroyed.

- Prayer: The Word says we can all come boldly before His throne. Prayer is an earthly, legal permit to heavenly intervention.

11. SPIRITUAL MEDICATION—THE TWO BEST ONES ON THE MARKET

The Medicine of God's Word

PLEASE UNDERSTAND THAT GOD'S WORD IS BETTER THAN THE BEST MEDICINE on Earth. It heals like no other, and it has no negative side effects. The instructions on the bottle must be followed in order for it to work; if it's not followed properly, there will be many problems. It has no expiry date and no prescription cost at the end of the treatment. This medication medicates deep into the root of the blood and cell production.

Like the natural medicine that we swallow, the Word must be applied through the mouth, ears, and eyes.

Strength:

> *For the word of God is quick, and powerful, and sharper than any two-edged sword, piercing even to the dividing asunder of soul and spirit, and of the joints and marrow, and is a discerner of the thoughts and intents of the heart.*
> —Hebrews 4:12

Ingredients: God Himself, God's breath; supernatural power; one hundred per cent God's Word.

Usage: Use three times a day and in addition as needed. You can never use too much— the more the better.

Deborah Nembhard-Colquhoun

Medicine Directives of God's Word

My son, attend to my words; incline thine ear unto my sayings. Let them not depart from thine eyes; keep them in the midst of thine heart. For they are life unto those that find them, and health to all their flesh.

—Proverbs 4:20–22

My son, attend to my words: Listen to the Word or God diligently, giving God your undivided attention. Focus on the Word of God. The key to healing is hearing. It's through hearing what the Word of God says that you will produce faith. Faith comes by hearing, and hearing by the Word of God.

Incline thine ear unto my sayings: Bending our ear down. Humility, bend your old habit, your own view, your own ideas, your negativity, what you knew before. And let God teach you.

Let them not depart from thine eyes: Focus your spiritual eyes and do not let God's Word or sayings leave your eyes.

Keep them in the midst of thine heart: Listen to the Word, hear the Word, and focus your eyes on the Word. Then the Word will program your heart. Meditate on the Word; memorize it, and it will stay deep in the core of your heart.

Why follow the directive? *For they are life unto those that find them, and health to my whole body.*

Take God's Word as medicine after every meal. Study it.

Prayer Medication

Usage: Pray without ceasing; pray always in the spirit. Three times a day dosage will produce great results. Apply it with the Word and faith.

Ingredients: Contains the active ingredients: boldness, authority, and Holy Spirit.

Prescription: Turn away from sin. *"Watch and pray, that ye enter not into temptation: the spirit indeed is willing, but the flesh is weak,"* (Matthew 26:41).

12. DEPARTMENTS THAT AID IN ONE'S WELL-BEING

Birthing and Deliverance

MANY PEOPLE ARE PREGNANT WITH A SPIRITUAL BABY. MANY HAVE HAD A stillbirth, and some have died spiritually during childbirth. Here at the Spiritual Hospital, we help people birth their destiny the spiritual way. I was pregnant myself and have gained experience both on a personal level through the teaching of Jesus and by going to a spiritual college.

As it is in the natural, so is it in the spiritual. Just as we are pregnant with a natural baby, we can also be pregnant with a spiritual baby. Many Christians are carrying visions, destinies, and dreams that God impregnated into them. Not only do they have to feed their baby with the right spiritual nutrition, they need to be educated in the birthing process.

Giving birth to one's destiny is like giving birth to a baby. Certain components must be present to ensure a healthy baby. In the natural birthing process, from conception to delivery, a healthy womb must be maintained to nurture and protect the baby. During the delivery process, there is intense pain or pressure during contractions, proper positioning of the baby, anxiety to see the baby born, and the cutting of the cord. It requires great power and strength!

The same is true in the spiritual birthing process. The spiritual baby requires a strong, healthy womb in which there is adequate nutrition and protection for proper development. The correct position of the baby is critical during natural child birth. If the baby isn't positioned properly, major problems can result. This is the same for a Christian. If the individual is not at the right place, they won't be able to give birth to their vision, which could result in a stillbirth. Courage and strength are also needed in the delivery process. If the individual doesn't have enough strength or courage to push the baby out, many problems will ensue. If a Christian lacks power, the spiritual baby (vision/destiny) will come to an end.

God has given all Christians enough spiritual power to give birth, but they need to understand how to use their power. If a baby is too large, it will need another type of intervention to be delivered. In the same way, the spiritual baby might be too large. In this case, others are needed to help in birthing forth the vision. Fear is another component. If during the process of giving birth the mother is fearful, this will prevent her from relaxing, which will cause the pelvic area to tighten up and delay the birth of the baby. The same is true in the spiritual realm; fear will cause a major delay in birthing a baby. After the baby is born, the umbilical cord must be cut. It's the same in the spiritual birth ... you have to cut your destiny or vision loose to release it into the Earth.

Spiritual Therapy Department
Many people are unaware of God's presence because they are messed up spiritually or have had spiritual accidents. These people are in need of therapy. We are now forming our therapy department, where you will learn how to understand the use of praise and worship as a form of therapy. Our healing could very well be locked up in our praise.

We're faced with many dilemmas in life, such as fear, depression, marital problems, financial problems, and other sources of stress. The influences behind most of these are demonic activities from the dark side of the supernatural world. Demonic spirits will rob us of the fulfilled life we are to live here in the natural. Later we will talk about how to overcome these demonic influences.

When we worship God, we're drawn out of the natural environment into the spiritual environment, where we will connect to God. If you allow yourself to focus completely on God in this realm, every one of your situations in the natural will become dim. It will release all your troubles and concerns so that you will experience joy, peace, and fulfillment that passeth all human understanding. Being in this atmosphere will strengthen your faith.

How Can Spiritual Therapy Help You?

- Help you discover meaning for your life.
- Bring you into the spiritual realm where you can connect to your life source (God).
- Broaden your natural understanding of yourself.
- Diminish your stress, anxiety, depression, and loneliness.
- Provide access to spiritual resources and weapons to defeat your situation.
- Increase self-esteem.
- Strengthen your relationship with Christ and others.

This department requires the music, songs, and an anointed worship leader for the Holy Spirit to flow through their performance and voices and saturate the atmosphere.

Spiritual Nutrition Department:
We provide the undiluted bread of life to individuals (the Word of God).

- spiritual nourishing food in accordance with God's plan as per scriptures
- spiritual food to members and visitors
- an active environment for learning and mentoring
- spiritual diets for different diseases
- continuous education and learning for members and visitors
- monitoring of foods that are being served on a regular basis for additives and false by-products.

Symptoms of spiritual malnourishment: stress, depression, anxiety, fear, loneliness, self-doubt, self-judgement, sleeplessness, confusion, hopelessness, cynicism, self-medication, addictions, repeat failure, and co-dependent relationships.

In the physical, we can identify with what it looks like to be physically malnourished. We can also be malnourished spiritually.

Spiritually Bad Food That We Should Avoid:

- contaminated words (containing sin such as malice, craftiness, hypocrisy, envy and insult)
- old milk (free watered down milk)
- false teachings
- worldly understanding and wisdom
- our own understanding of doctrines
- man-made religion
- "feel good" teachings

These teachings are not only found in the pulpits, but on TV and radio, and in Christian books and DVDs. This type of junk food only satisfies temporal spiritual hunger, but it leads to long-term spiritual health problems that can be detrimental. It may taste very good, but it lacks spiritual nutrients, doing more harm to the spiritual man than good. Over time, it will even affect the natural body. Please understand that the natural body is generated by the spiritual man. The natural body is a house, or a mold, for the spirit. Let's avoid eating spiritual junk food and instead feast on the bread of life that will give spiritual power and promote spiritual health.

Good Spiritual Food

Just as the body requires food for health, growth, and development, so does our spiritual body (mind and soul). Our wellbeing will be determined by the type of food we intake. Many Christians are attending churches but not eating a proper diet. Most of the diets served in churches today are religious junk food, loaded with artificial sweet words to make you feel good. These churches might be growing, but only religiously and carnally. The vital diet we need is the Word of

God. Jesus called this spiritual food the "bread of life." Please note that the bread of life, which is the Word of God, is a necessary spiritual food for sustaining life.

Contaminated Spiritual Food

Like natural food that can be contaminated with bacteria, spiritual food can be contaminated with spiritual bacteria. God has preserved His spiritual food (the Word) throughout the ages, but especially in these last days when many false teachers and false prophets are allowing the major bacteria (the enemy) to contaminate the food. This is why it's important to recognize real food, so that when bad food is served to us, we'll know it's not the real food. You might ask, "How do I know the real stuff?" You'll know it by eating it first-hand from the pages of the Bible and placing it into your spirit. These ingredients cannot be changed, but the Holy Spirit will make the necessary changes, spice it up for you, and create different diets out of the already-prepared food. We called this the "reamah word." People today have little appetite for solid food teaching; instead, they desire only the spiritual junk food that provides a quick formula for success.

Spiritual Diet Plan for Christians

"*But he answered and said, It is written, Man shall not live by bread alone, but by every word that proceedeth out of the mouth of God,*" (Matthew 4:4).

"*Thy words were found, and I did eat them; and thy word was unto me the joy and rejoicing of mine heart: for I am called by thy name, O LORD God of hosts,*" (Jeremiah 15:16).

First, we need a regular intake of spiritual milk.

Newborn Babies

New babies are immature and will develop over time. If they don't, we have a problem.

> *Wherefore laying aside all malice, and all guile, and hypocrisies, and envies, and all evil speakings, As newborn babes, desire the*

> sincere milk of the word, that ye may grow thereby: If so be ye have tasted that the Lord is gracious.
>
> —1 Peter 2:1-3

How Should Baby Christians Grow?
"But grow in grace, and in the knowledge of our Lord and Saviour Jesus Christ. To him be glory both now and for ever. Amen," (2 Peter 3:18).

Paul declared that the Thessalonians grew exceedingly in faith (2 Thessalonians 1:3), and he prayed that the love of those in the church at Philippi would abound more and more (Philippians 1:9).

Second, we need to grow into mature food.

> Of whom we have many things to say, and hard to be uttered, seeing ye are dull of hearing. For when for the time ye ought to be teachers, ye have need that one teach you again which be the first principles of the oracles of God; and are become such as have need of milk, and not of strong meat. For every one that useth milk is unskilful in the word of righteousness: for he is a babe. But strong meat belongeth to them that are of full age, even those who by reason of use have their senses exercised to discern both good and evil.
>
> —Hebrews 5:11-15

> And I, brethren, could not speak unto you as unto spiritual, but as unto carnal, even as unto babes in Christ. I have fed you with milk, and not with meat: for hitherto ye were not able to bear it, neither yet now are ye able. For ye are yet carnal: for whereas there is among you envying, and strife, and divisions, are ye not carnal, and walk as men?
>
> —1 Corinthians 3:1-3

How Should Mature Christians Grow?
"As newborn babes, desire the sincere milk of the word, that ye may grow thereby," (1 Peter 2:2). Milk is also important for mature babies, but in this case, it must be included with solid foods.

"... *grow in the grace, and in the* knowledge *of our Lord and Savior Jesus Christ,*" (2 Peter 3:18, emphasis added)

"*Man shall not live by bread alone, but by every word that proceedeth out of the mouth of God,*" (Matthew 4:4b).

The psalmist tells us to mediate on God's Word day and night (Psalm 1:2).

Spiritual Supplement

In addition to the real spiritual diet (direct from the Bible), we require spiritual supplements; these can be categorized as Christian books, CDs, and other resources. There are good ones on the market, but research and discernment are needed.

While it's important that you use discernment and seek direction from the Holy Spirit, these supplements will not provide the same spiritual health benefits as the primary diet (Word of God), but they will aid in the growth and development process. I would recommend that you not use them to substitute for the real diet, but rather use them in addition to the Word of God.

A more profound list of supplements was given to us in Scriptures (2 Peter 1:5-9) so that we could grow in grace and peace:

- moral excellence
- knowledge
- self-control
- patient endurance
- godliness
- brotherly affection
- love

If you're lacking certain nutrients in the natural realm, your body is at risk of developing certain diseases, and your growth and development is arrested. These supplements are spiritual boosters to prevent malnourishment.

Deborah Nembhard-Colquhoun

What to Eat When You Don't Feel Like Eating Directly from the Bible

- Take spiritual supplements three times per day as needed.
- Snack often throughout the day with short Christian books
- Keep ready to eat foods in your car, such as preaching and teaching CDs and Christian music. Turn your radio to the Gospel station. You can feast on the same at home. You can also play the Scriptures on tape, so you can hear it rather than read it.
- Attend good Christian preaching and teaching events.
- Be creative with your meal. Place it on your fridge at home or on your desk at work.

13. HOW DO WE RAISE THE DEAD?

THE BIBLE SAYS THAT AS BELIEVERS, WE ARE CAPABLE OF RAISING THE DEAD back to life (the physical body), as Jesus said we would do greater things than even he (John 14:12). The procedure to raise the dead is the same as that used to heal and deliver the sick. We rarely see the dead raised, but some stories have emerged from third world countries of people coming back to life. With this being said, there is yet another raising of the dead, which is the raising of the spiritually dead. This is of most importance, because it involves the eternal destiny of mankind. Let's look at why we need to raise a spiritually dead person back to life.

Mankind has separated himself from God, and as a result is spiritually dead and physically depraved. Romans 3:23 states, *"For all have sinned, and come short of the glory of God."* God didn't originally create mankind to be separated from Him. This separation caused mankind to become spiritually dead, physically depraved, and destined to die. *"Wherefore, as by one man sin entered into the world, and death by sin; and so death passed upon all men, for that all have sinned,"* (Romans 5:12).

How Did This Separation Happen?

In Genesis 2:17, God tells Adam that in the day he eats of the forbidden fruit, he will *"surely die."* This death refers both to spiritual death (Genesis 3:8) and physical death. Thus, mankind was spiritually dead at the original fall; however, physical death did not occur right away.

Deborah Nembhard-Colquhoun

How Can One Be Alive Again Spiritually?

When we are born again, spiritual death is rendered null and void. Physically, however, our bodies still die. "*And as it is appointed unto men once to die, but after this the judgment,*" (Hebrews 9:27).

Paul states in Ephesians 4:18, "*Having the understanding darkened, being alienated from the life of God through the ignorance that is in them, because of the blindness of their heart ...*"

We can only be alive again spiritually if we accept Christ as our Lord and Saviour. Colossians 2:13 says, "*And you, being dead in your sins and the uncircumcision of your flesh, hath he quickened together with him, having forgiven you all trespasses ...*" This Gospel needs to be preached to all mankind.

Mankind doesn't have the ability or the desire to reconnect to God, to overcome sin and death, or to bring himself from the state of spiritual death back to life. Only the supernatural, sovereign God can restore mankind. God knew this about mankind, which is why He sent Jesus Christ draw mankind back to Him. We must understand that salvation is God's work and that He redeems us as a part of His work. God made reconnection and new life possible at Calvary, but such life needs to come to fulfillment in us. God works continuously within us by rejuvenating our hearts. It's our duty to share the Gospel so that the work He started will be established.

Jesus came to Earth and died to redeem mankind back unto Himself. "*For God so loved the world, that he gave his only begotten Son, that whosoever believeth in him should not perish, but have everlasting life,*" (John 3:16). God doesn't want anyone going to Hell. Second Peter 3:9 states, "*The Lord is ... not willing that any should perish, but that all should come to repentance.*" One can truly come to repentance only through the Gospel. The Scriptures indicate that the way people come to be saved is through evangelization, by hearing the Good News of Christ, and then believing.

> *There is therefore now no condemnation to them which are in Christ Jesus, who walk not after the flesh, but after the Spirit. For the law of the Spirit of life in Christ Jesus hath made me free from the law of sin and death. For what the law could not do, in that it was weak*

through the flesh, God sending his own Son in the likeness of sinful flesh, and for sin, condemned sin in the flesh: That the righteousness of the law might be fulfilled in us, who walk not after the flesh, but after the Spirit.

—Romans 8:1-4

The apostle writes, "And you, being dead in your sins and the uncircumcision of your flesh, hath he quickened together with him, having forgiven you all trespasses," (Colossians 2:13).

14. WE MUST FOLLOW CHRIST

DURING HIS MINISTRY HERE ON EARTH, JESUS WENT ABOUT DOING THE GOOD work of the Father. He healed the sick, raised the dead, and cast out demons. These actions weren't natural—they were all supernatural. Why did Jesus have to do all this work? Couldn't He just come and die for our sins? Yes, Jesus could have come solely to pay the price at Calvary for our sinful nature. But what would we have learned from Him? He did an awesome job. We were able to see the supernatural manifested right before our eyes. God is indeed a wonder working God! We can do the same things, because we have the supernatural God living inside of us. If we manifest the supernatural God, then many will be able to perceive Him and come to follow Him. If He be lifted up, He will draw all unto Himself.

"*Let your light so shine before men, that they may see your good works, and glorify your Father which is in heaven,*" (Matthew 5:16). What light is this text talking about? It surely can't be referring to our flesh, because it wouldn't do much good in this spiritually dark world. It's talking about a supernatural light—Christ. The spirit of Christ is in all Christians; therefore, Christians should be demonstrating the supernatural attributes of the infinite God. Some of these attributes are righteousness, truth, love, and compassion. We should be performing many supernatural works, like healing, deliverance, miracles, signs and wonders, and conversions.

Christians aren't performing these supernatural works, however, because they are trapped in the natural realm. Flesh cannot perform supernatural works. It takes God in us to perform these works. God told us in His Word that we would do greater works after He sends us the comforter. The comforter came over two thousand years ago and dwells in those who are in Christ. How does He dwell in us? The comforter dwells in us through the anointing.

15. ALL BELIEVERS ARE GIVEN SPIRITUAL POWER

WHAT IS THIS SPIRITUAL POWER THAT ALL BELIEVERS WERE GIVEN? IT IS THE anointing. The word "anointed" means to rub. In the Old Testament, an individual was anointed with the rubbing of oil. Today we are anointed because Christ rubs himself on us and in us. God is a spirit; therefore, we are rubbed with His Spirit. To be anointed means to be set apart for a certain task. Since we are powerless, Jesus knew we would need His help to carry out His tasks. This is why Jesus sent us a comforter. The Holy Spirit's job is to work through us. He is the one who supplies the power. I would guess that by now most of us are aware that God has called and anointed us to do His will. My question is: Are we truly accomplishing the things of God by activating the power of the anointing?

There's a great need for the activation of the power in our personal lives, homes, churches, communities, and nation. We're in a crisis hour, a spiritual war zone in which people are dying every day. People are trapped in mental prisons, and disease is on the rampage. People are depressed, oppressed, and perplexed. Satan's troops have entered our churches and are warring against the believers. It's a shame that they're having a field day, but keep in mind that Jesus has told us in His Word that He will build His church, and the gates of Hell will not prevail against it (Matthew 16:18).

> *The Spirit of the Lord is upon me [us], because he hath anointed me [us] to preach the gospel to the poor; he hath sent me [us] to heal the*

brokenhearted, to preach deliverance to the captives, and recovering of sight to the blind, to set at liberty them that are bruised.
—Luke 4:18

Although this passage of scripture refers to Jesus Christ, it's applicable to us today. Jesus set the stage for us so that we could carry on with the mantle. In Christianity, there is only one body, and we as believers are part of that body—the Body of Christ. The word "Christ" means anointed. Christ is the Messiah, the Son of God, the anointed one. Everyone that is born again is anointed, because we are all in Christ. It doesn't matter how insignificant you may feel; you can rest assured that Christ is referring to you. You are special to God and are a part of the plan to carry out His task. He's not just referring to certain people, but to all His children.

In the past, limitations might have been placed upon you by others, even those in a high position in the church. Today I am here to let you know that the Word says you are anointed with the power that will enable you to preach the Gospel, deliver, and set free. It doesn't matter what people say ... if Christ says it, that settles it. You can't do anything by your own power, but with Christ, you can do endless things.

I experienced the power of God richly on my life a few years ago and had a deep desire to preach. I wasn't aware of the Scriptures, so I asked a pastor I knew if she thought I was called to preach, and she told me no. For years I refused to walk in the calling of God because I thought preaching wasn't for me. If I knew this truth then as I know it now, I would be farther along. Today your eyes have been opened, and you need not get a second option. Read the Word for yourself and believe that it is talking about you. It doesn't matter if you preach on the pulpit to a thousand or at the grocery store to only one, you are still called to preach, deliver, and set people free.

Before I continue, let's look at the word "power." Power is translated from the Greek word "durnamis," from which the English word "dynamite" is derived. The Holy Spirit gives us dynamite power that will explode from our lives into a world that needs such a glorious, heavenly explosion.

The Anointed Is the Spirit of God, Who Contains Power

Before we can understand the anointed power, we need to know its source. The text said that *"the Spirit of the Lord is upon me."* This is no ordinary spirit; the Spirit is God Almighty. The source of the power is God Himself in us and all over us. He is the source of all power, visible and invisible. He is the mighty God, the everlasting Father, the supreme God, the sovereign God, the deliver, the omnipresence God, and the God that caused the lightening to flash across the universe and the thunder to roll. He created the world out of nothing. This same God lives in our mortal bodies.

Not only do we need to know the source, but we also need to be aware of the God-given anointing power that is within us. We don't have to ask for the anointing power, because it's already within us. At "saving station" when we were saved, God transformed us into spiritual dynamite, a force to be reckoned with. You are armed and dangerous, because you are a carrier of a lethal substance (the anointing).

With the anointing power living in us, we have the power to heal, deliver, set free, and rescue people from the pit of Hell, bringing them into the marvellous light. We have the power to speak to our circumstances in the name of Jesus; we have power to tread upon serpents and lions. To destroy addictions, strongholds, and fear. We can go to the enemy's camp and take back everything he has stolen from us. We don't have to be afraid of anything.

If you don't believe that God has anointed you, I dare you to try it and see what happens. I tried it and was left speechless for three days. I was tired of doing things in the flesh and getting no results. Before I was to preach a mini sermon, I went before the Lord privately and asked Him to work through me. During the sermon, the power of God over took my entire body and worked through me, causing the people to experience His presence. They cried and were full of joy and glorifying God. People were set free because they testified to what God did that very hour. I didn't believe I was capable of doing such a work by letting the Spirit of God work through me. We have the power but must recognize it. Christ has spoken to us in Luke 4:18, and He has authorized us to exploit the power with the anointing. So start walking in it!

Jesus was anointed to do certain works and was aware of His anointing. He lived out that anointing in His life. Everywhere He went, He did great works. He preached the gospel to the poor; Luke 4:32 says, "*And they were astonished at his doctrine: for His word was with power.*" He healed the broken-hearted, He preached deliverance to the captives, and recovering of sight to the blind. He set at liberty them that were bruised. Can we say the same about us?

Before we take a look at the purpose of the anointed power, let's look at what's happing in our society. People nationwide are in despair because the forces of darkness are working hard against them. Principalities and powers and rulers of darkness in high places have set up their camp everywhere to fight against us. It's a disgrace that we are at ease in Zion. We're operating in a form of godliness, but we are denying the power thereof. Many of our motives when sharing the Gospel are wrong. It's all about me, myself, and I. We're seeking for fame, money, and power, and we have no concern for others. But it's not about us ... it's all about God. It's time we wake up, shake ourselves off, and do the will of God. We are to be a light in this dark world, but we've joined forces with the darkness.

We read earlier in Luke 4:18 that "*the Spirit of the Lord is upon me.*" This scripture gives us the purpose, which is to preach the Gospel and be a witness to its power. It's for work and service and to set the people free. We don't receive the anointing just so we can say that we have it, or to put it on a shelf like an unused item. The purpose of the anointing isn't to provide us with an emotional experience that shakes us in the Spirit so that we can have a good time without having a passion and love for the lost. It's not for speaking in tongue so that we might look powerful. It's to edify the Body of Christ; we cannot accomplish anything without the anointing. All of Jesus' miracles and healings were performed after He received the anointing.

God loves people, so that's the main purpose for the anointing. He stated clearly that we are to deliver and set others free. Although we also have the authority to set ourselves free, the text doesn't command us to set ourselves free, but to deliver others. We can't say we are anointed if we don't care about people or the winning of lost souls. The anointing gets results. We are to be a vessel, a channel of the anointing, allowing God to flow His anointing power through us to set people free and to bring deliverance and healing to the world around us.

There's no doubt that believers are equipped to fulfill this purpose, but we need to ignite the power. There are some dynamites sitting in the pews, singing in the choir, and preaching and teaching behind the pulpit, yet nothing is happing. Why? It's because they refuse to ignite the power. The Word of God reassures us that He provides the power to help us accomplish the task. It doesn't matter how good we can sing, preach, or pray—it's of no effect without the anointing. For the power of the anointing to flow, we must be plugged into the source. Light cannot shine unless it's plugged into the electrical source. So it is with the anointing. For it to work, it must be plugged into the supernatural, almighty power source (Jesus Christ).

How Do We Ignite the Power?

First, we have to get rid of every form of sin, because God is holy and will not connect to sin. When we are clean, we can go to God in prayer. Prayer is the key to igniting this power. It's the access key to the spiritual realm. If you look at Luke 4:18, you'll notice that Jesus spent much time in prayer and little time performing miracles. Jesus also went from one place of prayer to another place of prayer, and in between He performed miracles. Intimate time with God keeps the anointing strong on your life to minister to others. It's impossible to be in the presence of God without Him rubbing off on you.

Secondly, to ignite the power we need the Word. The Word is not just some word put together; it's the divine, inspired Word from God. There's something powerful about the spoken word. In scripture we read of a centurion servant who was terribly sick at home. Jesus just sent the word, and the servant was healed. We need to ignite the anointing by faith and send the word into the prisons, the hospitals, and this sick world; we have the power in the name of Jesus, but we have to use it for it to work.

Faith is another ingredient that ignites the power. Faith will allow the power of the anointing to manifest. We are trapped in our situation because we refuse to take a leap of faith. Let's build up our faith based on the fact that God has reassured us that His power is upon us to do great exploits.

The last ingredient we need is obedience. Faith without works is dead. How about stepping out by faith? The anointing is transferred through a point of contact in faith, believing you have received through that contact (most often the laying on of hands and prayer).

In Summary
How do we know that we are equipped with the power to make a difference? We are authorized by God to terrorize Satan's kingdom, to set people free, to break yolks, and to rescue people from the eternal dungeon, yet we refuse to obey. How much love do we show if we watch people dying spiritually, physically, and emotionally when we can make a difference? Maybe Satan has blinded our eyes so that we won't recognize our God-given power, but now we have been made aware and have no excuse. God has allowed you to read this text. Let us now do the will of the Master together by activating our spiritual power to wage a war against the enemy's army that has been defeating our lives, our churches, our schools, our government, and the nation. One will chase a thousand, but two will put ten thousand to flight. Jesus has already defeated Satan; however, most Christians don't realize that Satan is afraid of us, so we allow him to win battles.

Satan knows what kind of power we hold, which is why he blinds us to the truth. We are anointed and have been sent out by God to make a difference in this dark world. Let us walk in the Spirit so that when Jesus returns, He will not say, *"Depart from me, you who practice lawlessness,"* (Matthew 7:23, NASB), but will instead say, *"Well done, thou good and faithful servant,"* (Matthew 25:21).

How Christians Can Release Their God Given Power and Heal the Sick
Laying on of Hands
God has instructed us to lay our hands on the sick, and they will recover. God's power works through us and then flows to someone else

in the same way that electricity flows through copper wire. It's not the natural hands that cause the healing, but rather a transfer of God's power in the supernatural realm. Nevertheless, discernment is needed in everything we do. Please note that God also said in His Word not to lay hands on anyone suddenly.

Through Speaking the Word to the Disease
The Word of God is a powerful supernatural weapon that can cut through any spiritual situation; it works well with authority and faith. Jesus told us in Mark 11:23-24:

> ... *whosoever shall say unto this mountain, Be thou removed and be thou cast into the sea; and shall not doubt in his heart, but shall believe that those things which he saith shall come to pass; he shall have whatsoever he saith. Therefore I say to you, What things soever ye desire, when ye pray, believe that ye receive them, and ye shall have them.*

Through Agreement
There is power in agreement. The Word of God says that if two people agree on Earth concerning anything that they ask, it will be done for them by the Father in Heaven. For where two or three are gathered together in His name, He is there in the midst of them (Matthew 18:19-20).

Through the Name of Jesus
There is power in the name of Jesus. The Bible says that at the very mentioned of the name of Jesus, demons flee. The name of Jesus is a powerful, supernatural weapon against disease:

> *And whatsoever ye shall ask in my name, that will I do, that the Father may be glorified in the Son. If ye shall ask anything in my name, I will do it.*
>
> —John 14:13-14

Peter and John used the name of Jesus in their healing.

Silver and gold have I none; but such as I have give I thee: In the name of Jesus Christ of Nazareth rise up and walk. And he took him by the right hand, and lifted him up: and immediately his feet and ankle bones received strength. And he leaping up stood, and walked, and entered with them into the temple, walking, and leaping, and praising God.

—Acts 3:6–8

Through Prayer
The story found in Acts 3 provides an excellent example of the power of prayer.

Through Praise and Worship
The man healed in Acts 3 responded appropriately with praise and worship.

Formula to Receive Your Healing
You Must Be Born Again
First, you must be saved. Being saved removes you from under the curse that caused you to be sick in the first place. Jesus became a curse for you, so you don't have to live under the curse anymore. A spiritual blood transfusion happened when His blood was shed on Calvary for all mankind, and through this you are already healed. However, you have to know that it's rightfully yours and accept it by faith. The same process applies as when you accepted Christ as your Lord and Saviour. How will you accept healing and step up in faith if you don't know that it's God's will to heal you?

Repentance
God requires that we repent and turn away from any unconfessed sins in our lives. Once we confess these hidden sins, we remove any hindrance or blockage. Sin is a great blockage that closes the door to healing. God will not work on our behalf if we don't repent.

Forgiveness

Unforgiveness gives legal ground to the enemy. It opens the door to the spirit of infirmity, which causes all kinds of sickness and disease. For you to break the ground of unforgiveness, you must release the person that has done wrong towards you. It hurts, but it's better to release yourself than allow it to imprison you.

Laying on of Hands

"*And these signs shall follow them that believe ... they shall lay hands on the sick, and they shall recover,*" (Mark 16:17-18).

Speak to the Sickness

We were given authority to heal in the name of Jesus; therefore, we can speak by faith in the name of Jesus to the sickness, and it must obey. When we speak, it's just like Jesus is speaking through us, because we have the Spirit of God in us: "*Jesus saith unto him, Rise, take up thy bed, and walk,*" (John 5:8). Peter also demonstrated such faith and power: "*Then Peter said, Silver and gold have I none; but such as I have give I thee: In the name of Jesus Christ of Nazareth rise up and walk,*" (Acts 3:6). We have the same authority today.

Deliverance

In many cases, deliverance is needed before healing can take place. Many sicknesses are a result of the spirit of infirmity, and these spirits must be cast out before the deliverance can take place. The root cause of infirmity is often generational curses or spells. We must renounce them and repent of our sins. Often the ministry of deliverance is needed. Often when deliverance is performed, the healing automatically falls into place, or at least is very easy to apply.

People go through life with many problems, not realizing that they have contracted spiritual diseases from the person with whom they've had intercourse. When a person has multiple sex partners, they pick up spiritual demons and then pass them on to their next partner. Sex is a doorway for demons to enter an individual's body; therefore, we need to be careful whom we allow into our bodies.

16. HEALING AND DELIVERANCE

Healing through Deliverance (Matthew 8:16)
PEOPLE ARE SICK WITH MANY DISEASES, SUCH AS CANCER, DIABETES, HIGH blood pressure, and other ailments. Some of these can be categorized as generational demons. The spirits behind some of these afflictions are called "spirits of infirmity." A person can be healed of the spirit of infirmity through deliverance. The procedure we use in deliverance is the same that we use in the general procedures. Prayer points are provided further on in this book that will help in this process.

Spiritual Roots and Doorways to Physical Diseases
Those who are spiritually dead suffer from physical and spiritual diseases, such as diabetes, heart problems, cancer, migraines, ulcers, high blood pressure, poverty, demonic influences, possession and obsession, depression, addictions, and suicidal thoughts.

Sin opens the door to unforgiveness, worry, fear, stress and anxiety, disobedience, pride, anger, bitterness, jealousy, criticism, sexual immorality, curses, occult practices, trauma, rejection, loneliness, and guilt.

The remedy for all of this is salvation, forgiveness, repentance, renunciation, utilizing spiritual weapons, spiritual medication, spiritual nutrition, spiritual therapy, spiritual armour, and spiritual counselling,

Not All Physical Problems Are Related to Demons
Some sickness is due to the environment, poor diet, overeating, drug abuse, physical injuries, and other natural causes. These same

sicknesses can worsen and become severe due to demonic infestation. On the other hand, many diseases are related to demonic activity. In the same way that bacteria or germs enter a person and cause disease, demon spirits can enter a person and cause diseases and disabilities. The demons usually find entrance through sin or a generational curse. They afflict the person with different sicknesses, to the point of possessing the person's body. When people sin, they give the devil legal rights to enter their body or life.

Generational curses pass down through the family lineage. Their effect can be physical, emotional, mental, financial, or spiritual. This is why no matter how hard some people work, they always struggle with their finances, or are suffering from sorrow, sicknesses, and affliction. They are being attacked by demons. Without casting out the demons, they will remain afflicted, and it may even get worse. Deliverance is needed in these cases.

How to Drive out Demons that Cause Afflictions

Before driving out demons, you must understand that demons cannot live in a person without their permission. A demon that is living in a Christian is there by deception. When the deception is revealed and Christ is ruling in the person's life, then the demon spirit will have no choice but to go. A demon spirit that remains inside a person is either there because the person doesn't want the demon to leave, or the person has a mental condition.

Driving out Demons

Three things are required to cast out a demon. First, you need the permission of the possessed person. Secondly, that person must want deliverance, and thirdly, the deliverance must be done in accordance to the Word of God. Jesus himself demonstrated how we must conduct deliverance.

The first thing we observe in Jesus' ministry of deliverance is that He lived a clean life, walked in love, spent much time in prayer, and taught the people (Jesus emphasized teaching and preaching over driving out demons). Even when teaching in the synagogue, He expelled a demon. The people were amazed at His teaching, because He taught them as one who had authority. A man in their synagogue who was possessed by an evil spirit cried out to Jesus, asking what He wanted and if He had come to destroy him. He claimed to know that Jesus was the Holy One of God. We shouldn't have conversations with demons, because Jesus did not. Jesus told the demon to be quiet and come out of the man. The evil spirit shook the man violently and came out of him with a shriek (Mark 1:22-26). Jesus used His word to drive out the demons in Matthew 8:16: *"When evening came, many who were demon-possessed were brought to him, and he drove out the spirits with a word and healed all the sick,"* (NIV).

Demons are spirits and cannot be cast out by the flesh; therefore, we must draw upon the power of God, His Word, the blood, and Jesus' name. A born again believer is authorized to cast out demons, because God has given us the power to cast them out.

> *And the seventy returned again with joy, saying, Lord, even the devils are subject unto us through thy name. And he said unto them, I beheld Satan as lightning fall from heaven. Behold, I give unto you power to tread on serpents and scorpions, and over all the power of the enemy: and nothing shall by any means hurt you.*
> —Luke 10:17-19

According to Ephesians 2:6, we are seated with Christ in heavenly places. This means we are a rank above the demons and therefore have authority over them. Our authority is administered through faith with the spoken word directed at the unclean spirit. Although we have the authority to demolish strongholds, we cannot attempt it unless we are in total submission to God.

Prayer Points for Deliverance

For prayer points to be effective, you must know the Lord Jesus as your Lord and Saviour. You must say them aggressively, loudly, and with authority. First, you need to renounce every ungodly deed, and then ask God to forgive you. If you have unforgiveness towards anyone, you must forgive that person before you can go into deliverance. After this, you must apply the name of Jesus and the blood. It's always a good idea to curse the situation from the root through the blood of Jesus.

Renouncing Ungodly Vows

"In the name of Jesus, I repent and renounce any and all evil covenants, agreements, or promises that I made to Satan, and I ask that you will forgive me and release me from the bondage that any of these vow have brought upon me. In the name of Jesus, and by the power of the blood of Jesus, break and abolish them and send them back to the pit of Hell. I now declare that I am released from all ungodly vows and their bondage in the name of Jesus. I command any evil spirits that have attached themselves to this unholy vow to leave me now, in the name of Jesus."

Repeat this prayer for other issues and change the words "ungodly vows" to the issue you need to get rid of.

Breaking Generational Curses

"In the name of Jesus, I go into my generation lineage, and I confess the sins and iniquities of my parents and all other ancestors. In the name of Jesus, and by the power of His blood, I renounce, break, and destroy all cords of iniquity and generational curses that I have inherited from my parents and all other ancestors. In the name of Jesus, I free myself and my future generations from any generational curses that have passed down to me from my ancestors, and I command any evil spirits that have attached themselves to any of these cords of iniquity and generational curses to leave me now, in the name of Jesus.

Other sinful things that you can reject and renounce include:

- Any satanic ritual in which you were involved
- Any satanic assignment that was assigned to your life
- Any satanic spirits that were assigned to guide you
- Any authority you may give to Satan
- Your involvement in the occult, witchcraft, idolatry, or the psychic realm

17. SPIRITUAL COVERING

Proper Supernatural Covering as a Precaution to Prevent Body Damage

CHRISTIANS ARE SPECIAL TARGETS FOR THE ENEMY; THEREFORE, THEY MUST be protected spiritually from head to foot at all times, especially when going into the enemy's territory. We are facing a war zone of principalities, powers, the rulers of the darkness of this world, and spiritual wickedness in high places (Ephesians 6:12). If we aren't prepared, we become prey for the enemy. I urge all Christians—especially those who are going out with the Gospel—to be fully prepared, or else great consequences will result.

There are some Christians who are so spiritually unprepared to engage the enemy that they go onto the battlefield completely defenseless. No wonder they're easily defeated! In the physical world, a good soldier would never go into battle unprepared to engage the enemy; he would put on his protective equipment and carry his weapons. In the spiritual world, a Christian should never go into Satan's kingdom unprepared for battle. Through His Word, God has cautioned us about this war zone and provided the armour that is required to protect and equip His soldiers to fight against the enemy.

If we use the armour God provides for us effectively, not a single one of Satan's evil arrows will get through. We must put on every item properly, and also know how to use our divine weapons. This war will only be won in the power and might of the Lord.

Deborah Nembhard-Colquhoun

Belt of Truth
The complete protection that we need is the whole armour of God. We're first told to gird ourselves with the Belt of Truth. It's strange that God tells us to put on our belt before the rest of the war garments. In the physical realm, we usually put on a belt after all of our other clothing, but we're not dressing for a physical war zone. This is a supernatural war zone, and things are very different there. I'm not talking about Heaven, but right here on Earth. We currently live in the physical realm, but there is a spiritual realm around us. When we enter into this realm, we must have the right foundation. We must learn the truth and then know how to bind ourselves with this truth.

This piece of armour fastens all other parts of the armour securely together. Without it, the other garments won't stay intact. The many different cults, religions, and even those who profess Christianity, will twist the truth. If we don't know the truth, we will be fooled, twisted, and even converted to their beliefs—or at the very least, become confused. Even the real hope that we have will be lost; we won't even believe that we've been declared righteous. We'll stop trusting the Word, our faith will be damaged, we'll have no peace, and our relationship with God will change.

Breastplate of Righteousness
This piece of armour provides protection for our heart, and only those who are clean can wear it. Jesus will never put Himself into a dirty vessel. Righteousness covers and protects the Word of God in our hearts. The breastplate represents Christ's righteousness in us. We're declared righteous by the grace of God; however, we're required to maintain this righteousness. How do we do this? We do this by watching what we say, what we see, what we do, what we think, and where we go; everything should be Christ-based. If we keep our hearts pure and live a righteous life, Satan won't be able to touch us. If we're not covered with righteousness, Satan will search us out and know that we're powerless. He will ask us the same question he asked in Scripture: "*And the evil spirit answered and said, Jesus I know, and Paul I know; but who are ye?*" (Acts 19:15).

Righteousness Maintenance Tips

- Consult the maintenance manual (the Bible) before, during, and after conducting a service. Guidelines for maintaining righteousness can be found starting in the book of Genesis all the way to the end of Revelation.
- Perform a spiritual body wash with prayer and fasting on a regular basis. The Holy Spirit will perform the work for you.
- Disinfect from your head to your feet with the Holy Spirit at all times. The Holy Spirit dwells in the midst of sincere praise; therefore, it's a good habit to practice praise and worship.
- Spirit-proof yourself from every corrosion (sin).
- Perform a diagnostic check of yourself regularly in the Word.
- Attend the congregation that is in alignment with the Word of God.

Our Feet Shod with the Preparation of the Gospel of Peace
This peace is used to set people free from sin. We must be willing to go with the good news of salvation, wherever and whenever God leads us. This piece of armour will free people from the bondage that Satan has them in.

Shield of Faith
"*Above all, taking the shield of faith, wherewith ye shall be able to quench all the fiery darts of the wicked,*" (Ephesians 6:16). The shield is designed to protect us. When the enemy comes into our lives like a flood, we must have the faith to stand firmly on all of God's promises, believing that God is faithful and true to keep them. We might have the Word, but without faith, it won't work. The Word is the weapon, and faith pulls the trigger. We acquire this faith by hearing the Word of God. The Bible says that faith comes by hearing, and hearing by the Word of God (Romans 10:17).

Deborah Nembhard-Colquhoun

The Helmet of Salvation
The helmet of salvation guards our minds. Many Christian don't realize that spiritual warfare takes place in our mind. It's the battlefield where Satan concentrates most of his attacks. Satan uses our minds to distract us with carnal interests, the lust of the flesh, the lust of the eyes, and the pride of life. He's always persuading us to sin, and because we were once slaves to sin, we're vulnerable. Now that we have salvation, we're free from sin. We're no longer slaves, so we don't have to yield to Satan's tricks. Through it all, God is able to keep us in perfect peace, but our minds must be stayed on Him. When our minds are on Him, we will have the mind of Christ, which will enable us to resist and combat the enemy.

The Sword of the Spirit—the Word of God
We are fighting a spiritual war and are no match for the enemy. He will tear us to shreds. As Christians, we need a powerful weapon to combat the wiles of the devil. Our weapon can't be just any old thing, nor can it be the most powerful weapon devised by man. Our weapon is like no other—it's the unadulterated Word of God that is sharper than any double-edged sword, penetrating even to the point of dividing soul and spirit, joints and marrow (Hebrews 4:12).

This is the main offensive weapon we have in our collection; no other weapon can match it. The enemy will flee seven ways, confused at its very presence. This weapon is so powerful that it will cut through Satan's strategies and deceits. Out of it comes unlimited weaponry for every kind of war, in this world and in the spiritual realm. This weapon is fully equipped; it even has an advanced scope that can peer into the deepest part of Hell to see what tricks Satan is planning. With this insight, we can stay on Earth and fire a Holy Ghost missile or a spiritual laser beam right down into Hell. Jesus accomplished this while He was on Earth. One example of this occurred when He sent the word all the way to the centurion's home and healed the sick servant. If we have enough faith, we don't have to necessarily be present ... all we have to do is send the spiritual nuclear bomb (the Word) into the prison, the hospital, or even oversees. The Word is so powerful, it will go to Hell (the root of the cause) and then travel through the arteries of the spiritual world straight to the individual, and then complete the needed work.

Pray in the Spirit
The final piece of the armour is prayer. We need to pray! Pray, pray, and pray. Prayer in the Spirit happens when we allow our mind and spirit to maintain open conversation with God through the Holy Spirit. We're no longer praying in the flesh, but allowing the Spirit to pray through us. While we pray, we receive a spiritual injection to immunize us against the enemy's plots. This type of prayer is very effective in spiritual warfare, because even though we're spiritually limited, God is able to see and attack all things for us.

Sometimes we don't know what has happened in the spirit, but major damage has taken place. Do you know that many things are broken down and created in the spiritual realm when we pray in the Spirit? I've seen this happen many times. One experience I had happened while driving on the highway. God brought an elder to my mind, so I started praying in the Spirit, not knowing what I was praying. A couple of days later, I saw the elder and told him about the experience. He was astonished, because for years at his work place he'd been in a situation where they had refused to compensate him with money he was justly due. He told me that my prayer caused the funds to be released.

Another example of the power of prayer occurred during a time when my husband and I were praying in the Spirit. My husband, who sees open visions frequently, told me that while I was praying, he saw Heaven opened. A very bright light shone down through our roof, and billions of angels in white apparel stood around our entire living room, holding their swords. He said he was in awe experiencing such a sight; he even said that if he was not yet saved, that experience would have caused him to accept Christ, because it was so real.

If you're not equipped and anointed by God to invade and conquer some territory, stay put for your own good. There are devils and demons waiting in line to have a field day with you. However, if you're confident that you're well covered, then go wherever God leads you.

Please note that all born-again believers, not just those who call themselves "Christians," are armed and very dangerous and are able to terrorize Satan and his kingdom.

Once I was watching a television broadcast about an evangelist who was in Africa doing an open air crusade. During the crusade, a witch doctor come into the meeting to attempt to destroy him. While this witch doctor was talking and beginning to cast his spell, the evangelist felt the power of the Holy Spirit overtake him. Immediately, the witch doctor began having an asthma attack and had to run for his life. The evangelist didn't have to do anything, because the power of God was fighting for him. This is the power we have as believers. All we need to do is stay true, and God will lift up the standard for us.

Let us go and fight the good fight of faith, knowing that although we are flesh and blood, we have weapons of mass destruction (the Word of God and prayer) to wipe out the enemy's army.

> *For the weapons of our warfare are not carnal, but mighty through God to the pulling down of strong holds; Casting down imaginations, and every high thing that exalteth itself against the knowledge of God, and bringing into captivity every thought to the obedience of Christ.*
>
> —2 Corinthians 10:4-5

18. THE POWER OF PRAISE AND WORSHIP

MANY CHRISTIANS ARE LIVING A DEFEATED LIFE BECAUSE THEY HAVEN'T learned how to tap into the power of praise and worship. Praise and worship means to set aside our own agendas and press into God's presence, thanking Him for who He is and what He has done.

Even a sinner can praise God, but only a Christian can worship God. Worship is who God is. A sinner doesn't have the true understanding of who He truly is. When we worship God, we adore Him for who He is: the Great I Am, the mighty God, the everlasting father, the king of kings, the lord of lords, the creator, the sustainer.

How Do We Worship God?

The most common way to worship God is by expressing adoration through our actions, such as singing, clapping, shouting, and dancing. We're to worship in spirit and truth, which means with a sincere mind and an honest heart. Scripture teaches us that we worship God when we give ourselves totally over to Him. In Romans 12, we're instructed to offer our bodies as living sacrifices, holy and acceptable to Him, which is our reasonable service unto Him.

Life can become so hectic at times that we can be ungrateful or forgetful in our attitude towards God. Think back for a moment to a time before you were saved and deep sin and bondage controlled your life. Perhaps you'd been through a period of financial difficulty or sickness, or found yourself staring at an empty refrigerator with mouths to feed. Was it not God who pulled you out of your distress? This should put praise and worship in our hearts and on our lips.

In many churches today, true praise and worship is either nonexistent or slowly dying. Look around at the world and see people praising and shouting on TV shows, dancing at concerts, or cheering at their favourite sporting event, yet many people who profess Christ as their Lord sit idly in the pews. As a pastor, I don't understand why people sit quietly when God's presence fills an entire room, especially when there's liberty to shout, dance, praise, and worship. I don't know about you, but like David in the Bible, I will bless the Lord at all times. His praises will continually be in my mouth.

God Wants Our Best Sacrifices

When you can praise the name of Jesus during both the good and bad times in your life, you're making a sacrifice. True sacrifice will cost us something. It takes you out of your comfort zone, causing you to give up and deny yourself. There are times when we are down and depressed, especially if things aren't going too well. Maybe we're experiencing a hardship or tragedy, and we don't want to thank God. Do you think Job felt like praising God when he lost everything? Job lost his family, his home, his possessions, and his health, all in one fell swoop. What does the Bible say he did? He worshipped.

"Naked came I out of my mother's womb, and naked shall I return thither: the Lord gave, and the Lord hath taken away; blessed be the name of the Lord," (Job 1:21). God asks some of us for our best sacrifices, just like He asked Abraham. But instead of offering Isaac, we offer Ishmael. This isn't what God wants; He wants the best, without spot, wrinkle, or blemish.

What Is the Power of Praise and Worship?

Every human being was created to live in an ideal environment—the presence of God—but sin robs us of that privilege. Praise and worship releases the supernatural power of God in our presence so that we can experience victory, joy, peace, breakthroughs, freedom, fulfillment, healing, and deliverance. It's a real eye-opener into the spiritual realm.

For example, metal that's in a moist environment will start to rust and eventually break down. Outside of our ideal environment, we face every kind of defeat from our adversary, Satan. God inhabits the praises of His people, so when we praise and worship Him, His presence will descend amongst us, filling every situation that we face and allowing us to experience success in our battles.

Praise Is a Weapon
The weapon of our warfare is not carnal, but mighty in pulling down every work of the enemy. You might be going through some tough stuff, but I dare you to praise the Lord. The children of Israel faced many battles, but they praised the Lord. When they did, they experienced victory. Christians are armed and dangerous, but we won't benefit from that until we begin to utilize and release our power. One of the weapons we have at our disposal is praise and worship. In Acts 16, Paul and Silas were beaten, chained, and locked up in the inner dungeon. At midnight, they were praying and singing hymns to God, and the other prisoners were listening to them. Suddenly, a great earthquake shook the prison and they were loosed of their chains. The prison doors opened and they were set free. This happened because they utilized their spiritual weapons.

19. GENERAL TIPS TO LIVE A FULFILLED LIFE

YOU MUST FIRST BE BORN AGAIN BY WATER AND SPIRIT. THIS WILL CERTIFY you as a child of God. Live in obedience according to the Word of God. Once you are a child of God, you're entitled to all His inheritance. For you to know and benefit from the inheritance, you must read the Word, study the Word, and do what the Word says. Do good, and good will follow you; give, and it shall be given unto you, pressed down and running over. Wear the whole armour of God, and you'll be protected from the adversary; be merciful, and you will obtain mercy. Be peaceful with others, and you will be at peace; stay away from sin (fire), and it won't burn you. Bless them that cure you, walk by faith and not by sight. *"Trust in the Lord with all thine heart; and lean not unto thine own understanding. In all thy ways acknowledge him, and he shall direct thy path,"* (Proverbs 3:5-6). Yes, these are all in the Word ... and much more!

Because you live in a fallen world, you'll often face negative situations, but just for a season. You may worry, but worry will fade away when you hear God's voice. God's voice makes a difference; His voice will give you assurance, direction, comfort, and hope, which in turn will produce peace, joy, and happiness.

To live a fulfilled life, you must endeavour to be in God's presence. Understand who you are in Christ, your power and authority, and how to connect to the spiritual realm and know what God's will is for you. You'll be fulfilled when you know for sure that your life is secure in God's hands. Trouble, testing, and persecution might come at times, but when you know that, *"all things work together for good to them that love God, to them who are the called according to his purpose,*" (Romans 8:28), nothing should stop you. If God is for you, who and what can be against you?

20. MINISTRY INFORMATION

AT SPIRITUAL HOSPITAL, WE DON'T WANT TO OPERATE LIKE TYPICAL CHURCHES, but instead operate more like a hospital, in a spiritual sense, working to make a difference in the lives of individuals.

Vision/Mission

We are a collaborative committee that encompasses the love of Christ and the power of the Holy Spirit to teach, educate, baptize, disciple, heal the sick, mend the broken-hearted, and break the chains that hold us back from the love of God. This is the Great Commission that we have employed in order to be an illustration of Christ.

We are dedicated not only to saving the lost and healing and delivering people through the power of Jesus Christ, but also to enhancing believers' spiritual knowledge by educating them about the role of the Word of God in their lives and showing them how to apply its principles in order for full manifestation of healing to take place. In scripture, one will discover insights that will provide guidance for life, and healing for mind, body, and spirit.

Our Method

The spiritual intervention team is commissioned to use nothing but the anointing power and gifts of the Holy Spirit. We utilize God's Word, love, compassion, faith, authority, and the power of prayer to cut down and root up any unclean issues.

The Spiritual Hospital is:

- a place where people are walking in the blessings of God
- a place where people are brought into a new and closer relationship with Jesus Christ
- a place where the Word and nothing but the Word is taught
- a place that helps people discover God's calling upon their lives
- a place where people's skills and talents are identified, encouraged, fine-tuned, and put to use for the Kingdom
- a place that equips people and commissions them to implement God's calling and mission on their lives
- a place that connects with the community, identifies issues, and works together to make a change

We also offer:

- encouragement and support
- mentorship, education, and training
- healing and deliverance
- spiritual and physical assistance
- support for loss and grief
- one-on-one visits
- a biblical view for adults, teens, and children who are dealing with illness, pain, grief's and other difficult issues
- Bible studies
- spiritual retreats
- individual consultations and counselling
- special events and social events
- open prayer hour
- training for more effective ministry
- home and phone prayer/prayer meeting upon request

All services are provided free of charge.

21. ENCOURAGING MINI-SERMONS

The Good News—the Gospel

THIS SERMON WAS PREACHED AT SPIRITUAL HOSPITAL AND AIRED ON YES TV in April, 2016.

"*For God so loved the world, that he gave his only begotten Son, that whosoever believeth in him should not perish, but have everlasting life,*" (John 3:16). I'm here to talk to you about the good news—the Gospel, the Kingdom of Heaven, the Kingdom of God—that is available to us, even while we're here on Earth. The Kingdom of God is available to us for eternity. Amen! In that kingdom there will be no sickness, no pain, and no suffering. All will be goodness.

I'll be taking my text from the Gospel and focusing on the resurrection, since it's resurrection Sunday. But before I go there, let's just take a walk down memory lane and recall how Jesus Christ came to Earth.

Over 2,000 years ago, Jesus Christ came as a baby and grew into an adult. The Word of God tells me that everywhere He went, He did good. He healed the sick, raised the dead, cast out demons, and preached the Gospel—the good news—with miracles, signs, and wonders. He did this to set an example for us as believers.

What is required of us? What should we be doing? The church should be demonstrating the Gospel—not just preaching the Word, but demonstrating the Gospel. We should see healings taking place everywhere, just as we are here at Spiritual Hospital. We know that God is able to heal. We aren't just preaching healing, we aren't just preaching blessing ... we're preaching and seeing demonstrations of what we are preaching. Amen!

The Bible says that God performed many miracles while He was on Earth. He took a little boy's lunch—five loaves of bread and two fish—and supernaturally multiplied them and fed thousands of people. Glory to God! I'm talking about the miracle working power of God. How He can take something little, exponentially multiply it, and turn it into something supernatural. This can't be done in the physical. That is the God I'm talking to you about this morning. He did so many miracle, signs, and wonders. He healed crippled people and all the sick people that came to him. He never turned anybody away. He even provided salvation. He did so many wonderful miracles over 2,000 years ago.

Jesus moved with compassion. Do you have compassion this morning? Are you touched with the feelings of the infirmities of others? Of those that are suffering, those that are broken, those that are on the street? Those that are messed up? Well, Jesus moved with compassion, and He did something about it. He went around healing and delivering. Because of His compassion, He was touched with the feelings of infirmities, of situations, of conditions.

So many people around us are messed up. Since we have the Holy Spirit in us, we should be touched with the feelings of others' infirmities and struggles. But are we really touched with the feelings of those who are suffering? I am challenging you this morning. Are you touched with the feelings of individuals' infirmities and afflictions? Can you feel their pain? Can you feel their suffering? Can you feel their longing? Can you really feel it? Jesus was touched with the feelings of those who were suffering.

This is why Spiritual Hospital is here to help the less fortunate, to help those that are bruised. Help those that are confused, those that are messed up, those that don't know what to do. Help those that are trapped in mental prisons and situations that they can't get out of. We should be so touched with the feelings of others that we want to do something about it. We don't want to just look at it and laugh and say "let them suffer." If you're touched with the feelings of somebody's infirmity, you want to move with compassion. Glory to God!

Many people are anointed; many people have the power of God, but they do nothing with it. This morning I want to challenge you to be touched with the feelings of somebody's infirmities and moved with compassion like Jesus was.

Do you know what Jesus was doing on Earth? He was showing you what you are to do. A lot of people have big titles and want to say, "OK, I am a big prophet; I am a big pastor." I am all that, but Jesus was only a servant. He came to serve and not to be served; He came to help the broken. Do you want to know what a true shepherd is? Do you want to know what a true pastor is? Those who can look at the people who are suffering and help them.

It takes the Lamb, the sacrificial blood of the spotless Lamb, to atone for your sins. It's done; all you have to do is believe it and receive it. Glory to God! It's free ... it is free! Glory to God! Although it appeared that man killed Christ, the Bible tells me that we fight not against flesh and blood. When the enemy comes at you in bodily, human form, understand that you're not fighting the actual person. Behind every fight and every trial there's an enemy, and the enemy is Satan. Glory to God!

God fought the battle on the cross for you and me. They crucified Him, and then they buried Him in the grave. The enemy thought, "I got Him now." There must have been a celebration going on in Hell. Yes, they must have been celebrating in Hell at that point when they buried Him, but it isn't over until it's over. While He was down in Hell, he terrorized Satan's kingdom. Who has the last laugh now? He was tied up into death, but He took it back.

You don't have to die ... you can live eternally, but only if you accept Jesus Christ as your Lord and Saviour. You don't have to die, because the Word of God tells me in 1 Corinthians 15:51:

Behold, I shew you a mystery; We shall not all sleep, but we shall all be changed, in a moment, in the twinkling of an eye, at the last trump: for the trumpet shall sound, and the dead shall be raised incorruptible, and we shall be changed.

Deborah Nembhard-Colquhoun

I feel the Holy Ghost. I feel the Holy Ghost deep down in my soul. Deep down in my whole being. Excuse me this morning if I look crazy to you, but I can't contain it. I can't be still, but I got to move, because fire shut up in my bones, and if I don't move, I will explode. I will burst, because I can't contain it. Glory! This is why the grave couldn't hold Him down. Oh glory to God! I feel like I'm intoxicated with something. I feel like I am on a high.

You know, when the disciples were in the upper room and they looked crazy, Peter explained that they weren't drunk, but they were filled up with the Holy Ghost. It's the Holy Ghost upon me right now. I feel like dancing. I feel like skipping. I am not drunk, but I am intoxicated with the power of the living God. People take drugs and alcohol to give them a high. Well, let me tell you that this high is nothing compared to the alcohol and drugs, because I feel sweet. I feel like jumping. I feel like skipping, because all my troubles are gone. I don't have any trouble. I came in this morning packed up with troubles, but they disappeared right about now. The Holy Ghost is in my spirit and He intoxicates me; He gives me a high. Somebody need a high. Somebody need a high from God. Glory to God!

When Jesus was raised from the dead, He told the disciples not to leave Jerusalem, but to tarry. Until what? Until they were imbued with power. Not dopey power, not voodoo power, not satanic power, but power from on high. Resurrected power, Holy Ghost power, and supernatural power. Heavenly power that will transform you and change you.

My God, how do people without the Holy Ghost manage? How do they live? I couldn't live if I hadn't been filled with the Holy Ghost. For those who are not filled, I am telling you this morning that you need to be filled. When the pain and sorrow hit you, you need a joy, you need a comforter ... and the comforter is Jesus. It ain't Spiritual Hospital. It ain't Deborah, but it's the Holy Ghost. Worry cannot stay in the presence of the Lord. Right now, worry cannot stay here; sickness cannot say here.

When I came here early this morning I didn't have a word for you. Fear started to hit me. But when the Holy Ghost took a hold of me, fear was kicked out. Glory to God, it was kicked out because of the Holy Ghost. There is something about the Holy Ghost. When you have the Holy Ghost, you don't have to be calling up the pastors every minute and asking them to pray for you. Even if you do call them, it's just an outlet for you to be plugged into. That's why we come to church, so that iron can sharpen iron.

Last week, I was going through the same dimness, but something just plugged in. It was the Holy Spirit. Like a lamp that had been disconnected, I plugged into the source. When I plugged in, all the demons, all the spirits that wanted to lurk in the atmosphere and keep me down, had to flee, because demons cannot stay in the presence of God. They got to move. So it is with the demon that is causing your afflictions, the demon that is causing your pain. He cannot stand in the presence of the Holy Ghost.

Some of the afflictions you're going through aren't physical; they're spiritual sicknesses, but when you're imbued with the power from on high, they got to go. The sickness got to go; cancer got to go; high blood pressure got to leave you; arthritis has to leave you. Depression has to leave you; it cannot stay in the presence of the Holy Ghost, because where the presence of the Holy Ghost is, there is liberty and there is healing. In the presence of the Holy Ghost, demons tremble.

At Spiritual Hospital, we're going to change up our method of deliverance. I'm sick and tired of people and pastors coming before demons and saying, "Out, out, out!" We don't have to do that, because when the Holy Ghost is present, and with the authority that we have (the authority that was stolen from us), those demons in individuals must go. They have to take orders. They can't stay; they must listen to us, because when we speak, it's the Holy Ghost speaking. It is Jesus in me, speaking through me.

My sheep, understand that all the power that the enemy had before is broken. He is stripped of everything. My God! He is only powerful if you allow him to be. He is only powerful if you believe him to be. But if you understand the power of the resurrected Lord, you'll understand the power that lies within you as believers. My God, the Bible says signs and wonders shall follow. He didn't day "maybe;" He didn't say "if." He said signs and wonders shall follow the believers. Not the pastors, not the bishop, but the believers.

Who here is a believer this morning? Can I see the hands of the believers? Then why are sings and wonders not following you. Maybe you need to be plugged into the source. Maybe you need to be plugged into the electricity source, but if there is sin in your life, you cannot be plugged in. The Bible tells me that Jesus is all righteous, so if iniquity is in your heart, He will not hear you. Glory to God! He can't come near iniquity, so you need to go before God and confess your sins, even if you don't think you've sinned. Just tell Him your sins, and He is just and able to forgive you of all your sins and cleanse you of all unrighteousness (1 John 1:9).

You can't be righteous on your own, or through a man, or through the priest. You can only be righteous through Christ ... through the precious blood of Jesus. Glory to God!

My God Almighty, I want to teach, but it looks like I can't teach this morning. Glory, glory, glory! I am not here to entertain nobody. I am not here to entertain you, but I am here to stir your being. I am here to stir your spirit. For you to understand the Christ that is within you. Because greater is He that is in you than he that is in the world. You have got resurrection power. The same power that raised Christ from the dead is in you and me this morning, but you have to activate it. How do you activate it? By faith! Everything in the Kingdom of God operates by faith. You came to Christ by faith; you are living this walk by faith. For your activation to happen, you got to believe and reach out to Jesus, and He will plug you in. It's that simple.

My God! I need you to understand that Jesus did rise from death to life. What evidence do I have that he rose? Hallelujah! Many people wonder and speculate about the resurrection, and some people don't have faith in it. They say it never really happened, but it did happen! Hallelujah, glory to God!

If Jesus didn't rise from death, your Christian walk is in vain. Mighty God, I come against every spirit right now that will prevent your people from hearing and understanding the Word and retaining this word, God. I pray against every principality and every power and every satanic work that's trying to manipulate this message and prevent your people from believing the truth this morning, mighty God. I seal their minds, God, and their ears with your Holy Ghost fire right now, God Almighty. May your Holy Ghost fire consume every other spirit of influence in their ears this morning, God, so that they will hear the Word.

The Christian church rests on the foundation of the resurrection. The death is important; the cross is important, but if He didn't rise from dead, He would be just like the other religious figures. He would be just like Buddha; Buddha never rose from the dead. Allah never rose from the dead; Krishna never rose from the dead. But our Saviour, Jesus Christ, rose from the dead.

It was not a dopey ... you know, dopey as we say it in the Caribbean. It was not a spirit or a ghost. It was the resurrected body that I just talked about. The incorruptible body that you and I are going to change into, with no more sickness. How do I know that Jesus rose from the dead? The empty tomb! The stone was rolled away! The jailers were confused; they were not there. How do I know that Jesus Christ rose from the dead? The clothing that was on Him was intact, in the same position, but the body was not there. Glory to God! Only the supernatural God could have done something like this. This is why He is the only God that really rose from the dead.

If He hadn't risen from the dead, we wouldn't have true joy; we wouldn't have any true peace. If he hadn't risen from the dead, I would be coming to you every Sunday and preaching a lie. But He did rise. There is much evidence that He rose. Glory to God! Thomas would not believe that He rose. Thomas that was with Him, but he asked Jesus to show him the evidence— the nail print in His hand, so He showed it to Thomas. Thomas saw the nail prints in His hands. He saw His pierced side, and I'm sure he saw the nail marks in His feet. There were over 500 eyewitnesses to Christ's resurrection.

In this day, if a crime is committed with 500 eyewitnesses, that person will be found guilty. Think of the thousands of people who came to Christ because of the resurrection. Peter betrayed him by denying Him, but when he saw the risen Christ, he was willing to be crucified upside down for Him.

All the disciples went through agony. Why would they do that for someone who never rose form the dead? That doesn't make any sense. They were beaten; they went through so much because they believed when they saw the evidence. After His resurrection, Jesus went and ate with them and spoke with them. He showed Himself to so many people, including Paul on the road to Damascus.

Many people, such as Muslims and Hindus, have never heard the Gospel, but Jesus has revealed Himself to them just as He did with Thomas. My husband experienced such evidence. His spirit left his body, and he saw the nail prints. He saw them. That is why he is saved today. Many people saw it; they experienced it. If Christ didn't rise, who is this living within me? I can feel him; He is tangible within my spirit. If Christ didn't rise, how do you explain the many miracles of the Gospel? How do you explain the transforming power of the Gospel?

My joy is the Lord, my peace is the Lord, and my happiness is the Lord. The world can't give me this happiness; the world can't give me this joy. But the resurrected Lord lives within my soul. Glory to God! He woke me up this morning. He allows me to preach to you when I have no ability. The resurrected Lord, the resurrected Lord. He lives, He lives, He lives.

The Purpose to Change

This sermon was preached at Spiritual Hospital and aired on YES TV in November, 2015.

The Son of God appeared for this purpose, to destroy the works of the devil," (1 John 3:8, NASB). Jesus was on a mission to do something. He finished the work over 2,000 years ago. Mission accomplished.

How Did He Destroy the Works of the Enemy?

Jesus became sin for us so that we would be the righteousness of God. Jesus became the curse so that we would die with the curse, but when He rose, He rose without the curse. It is no longer I that live, but He that lives in me.

What Did Jesus Come to Destroy?
Jesus came to destroy all the works of the enemy, which includes sin, sickness, oppression, poverty, condemnation, and fear. He became poor so we can be rich. God doesn't give us the spirit of fear; there is no condemnation to those that are in Christ. He was wounded for our transgressions.

If Christ Came to Destroy the Works of the Enemy, Why Are We Still in These Conditions?
Although Christ came to destroy the works of the enemy, we all still live in this fallen, sinful world. The enemy is like a roaring lion, seeking whom he may devour. Satan is working overtime to destroy humans, but Jesus went to Hell and took back the power that death held over us. All power and authority was given to Jesus, and those of us who are in Christ have been given this power so that we can heal, change, and influence.

The Hand of God
This sermon was preached at Spiritual Hospital and aired on YES TV in March, 2015.

The following are some of the reasons why we all need the hand of God in our lives.

- You are limited in many things without the hand of God.
- You are going through some type of situation and are desperate for help.
- You are suffering, in pain, afflicted, poor.
- You are the victim of curses, spell, vexes, and generational issues.
- A friend or relative may be going through a tough situation and you are unable to help.
- You have tried to figure things out through your own efforts or abilities and have been unsuccessful.

What you need are the hands of God in your life. He specializes in the things that are impossible. He will do what no other power can do. His hands are like none other. Please understand that I'm not referring to a physical hand, but a metaphoric hand. God is a spiritual being; He is infinite and sovereign, but for our finite minds to understand Him, we must explain Him in the physical sense. "The hand of God" is a figure of speech used to describe the works of God. We are using symbolic language to convey some elements of truth about God, such as His power, actions, movements, protection, guidance, creativity, and presence.

I want to focus on God's hands in the general sense, and God's hands extended. We know that God created the world by speaking it into being. By our logic, we can say:

- God laid the foundation of the earth by His hands. He created the world by His hands.
- He took the sun and the moon and placed them into the sky and made light.
- He took the bone from Adam's rib and made a woman.
- He sprinkled some spiritual seed on the earth and it turned into trees, plants, and grass.
- Lay your hands on me, Jesus. I don't mind. Make me, mold me, and transform me.

You might not be able to see His hands working in the physical, but I see Him working in my life. He woke me up this morning by His hands. I can see His hands working a miracle in my hands. If someone hurts me, I leave it in the hands of God. My life is in the hands of God. I am limited, but I told God to hold my hands and lead me on. I have made it this far by the grace of God's hands.

God uses mankind's hands as His hands extended; He uses human hands as an extension of His own. God has given humans dominion over the earth and all that is in it; however, He knows we are limited and will need His help. Many people are taking credit for doing things, but it's really God working through them.

Spiritual Hospital is not ours; it's God's hands extended to the nation of Canada to bring healing and hope. In our hands we have the

Word of God, enabling us to proclaim the good news to the nation and this dying world. The world may see us as simple people, but we are doing some extraordinary things. You want to know our secret? It's not our abilities ... it's the hands of God working through us. He has placed spiritual weapons in our hands. The weapons of our warfare are not carnal, but mighty in pulling down strongholds. God has given us weapons to heal, to restore, to mend the broken-hearted, and to set at liberty those that are bruised.

Many Christians miss out on blessings because they are looking to man or trusting in their own abilities, power, or skills rather than trusting in God. God does not call and equip those that are prideful, but those that humble themselves.

We Are God's Extended Hands

God has called us to be His extended hands to help those that are hurting, confused, and lost find the right path to Him. Appearing before Moses in the burning bush, God called him to be the deliverer of Israel out of Egypt. Moses felt that he was unable to do what God had asked of him, so God took a shepherd's rod and empowered Moses. In the same way, God wants to empower us to do His work. He will help you destroy your enemy, part your Red Sea, perform miracles, or deliver nations.

With the hands of God, Joshua used a little spear to fight through the wilderness to get the children of God across the Jordan River. David used a little sling shot, but he used it in the name of God and knocked out the great giant, Goliath. There are some Goliaths in your life, and you need to use our little sling to defeat them.

You may be going through a financial crisis right now; your cupboards might be empty, or you may be living from paycheque to paycheque, but God's hands can transform all that. You may only have a little, but God can transform it. Jesus only had a little boy's lunch in His hands, but he took it and fed a multitude.

We serve a miracle working God who can take nothing and turn it into something. God will take your mess and turn it into a message; He will take your pain and turn it into joy. He will take your sickness and transform it into health. God will also take someone the world has rejected and clean them up, turn them around, and set their feet on higher ground.

You Weren't Created to Be in Sickness
This sermon was preached at Spiritual Hospital and aired on YES TV in April, 2015.
Our Scripture reference will be taken from Genesis 1:26-27, 31.

And God said, Let us make man in our image, after our likeness: and let them have dominion over the fish of the sea, and over the fowl of the air, and over the cattle, and over all the earth, and over every creeping thing that creepeth upon the earth. So God created man in his own image, in the image of God created he him; male and female created he them. And God saw everything that he had made, and, behold, it was very good.

Two questions that I will be addressing today are: What causes sicknesses? and, How can you be healed?

Many people embrace sickness because they believe that it's God's will for them to be sick. It has become part of their lifestyle. They can't see themselves being healed, and they can't see a way out. Many people use the Apostle Paul's experience of the thorn in his flesh to justify their sickness, or they look to the story of Job for justification, while overlooking the restoration God gave to Job.

You might think that you're completely healthy, or you might be physically sound, but you could be suffering from a broken heart, a broken relationship, or a difficult financial situation, which is also a form of sickness. If you've never been through any sickness, believe me—your time is soon coming. Sickness is no respecter of persons.

Sickness is real, and everyone will experience some kind of sickness in one form or another throughout their lifetime. It doesn't matter who you are, whether you are black, white rich, poor ... sickness it is no respecter of persons. You can try to prevent sickness, but certain types you can't stop; they will just attack you without permission. Some sicknesses will heal fast; some will take very long, while others never heal, all because we are living in a depraved world.

The unbelieving world struggles to understand the misleading and often confusing statements of how sickness came into our world. Sickness has been blamed on the environment, with many believing that if we preserve the earth, then sickness will be destroyed. Society also believes that sickness comes from genetics, bacteria, and viruses. If we could just get rid of those things, everything would be fine. This is why medical associations spend years developing new drugs to eradicate all of the viruses.

Even God gets the blame for our sickness. Many people cry out, "Why God?" God doesn't cause any of our sickness, but if you play with fire, you'll get burned. God can and will help, but you need to understand His laws. Take gravity, for instance. Try jumping off a cliff and see what happens; the law of gravity takes effect. All of these are contributing factors to sickness, but the real cause goes even deeper.

Sickness is not only physical; it can be spiritual, mental, emotional, and physiological. As a matter of fact, the root cause of most sicknesses is spiritual. Our medical system is designed to heal the physical part of human sickness, like cuts, injuries from accidents, drug and chemical abuse, alcoholism, or something as simple as poor eating habits, which are all part of the natural world and require natural solutions. Doctors are a blessing from God, who has given them wisdom, knowledge, and understanding of our natural illnesses. Most people, however, will go to a doctor to be healed from a sickness that can only be healed through a spiritual intervention. Due to a lack of knowledge, people will go and visit a physic, a witch doctor, a voodoo doctor, and the obi man, all of who deal with the dark side of the spiritual world. What we really are in need of is the supernatural divine intervention of almighty God.

Why Do We Have Sickness?
Sickness has may natural causes, but the number one root cause is sin, which has many elements. Through disobedience, we get sin from the enemy. You are a spirit who lives in a body, and you have a soul (mind, will, and emotions). Demons can't enter into the spirit of a person, but

they can enter and attack your soul and body. Sin in a person's life opens the door for a spirit to enter and inflict mental torment or disease.

Jesus had to rebuke a foul spirit, saying unto him:

Thou dumb and deaf spirit, I charge thee, come out of him, and enter no more into him. And the spirit cried, and rent him sore, and came out of him... But Jesus took him [the child] by the hand, and lifted him up; and he arose.

—Mark 9:25b-27

Why can a demon use disease to afflict a Christian? Once you sin as a Christian, you're no longer under the protective umbrella of God's grace. You're under the curse of the law, which gives Satan legal right to have one of his demons afflict you with a disease or an affliction.

The World Is Not Too Sick for God to Heal.

We have established what causes sicknesses, but now we need to establish how we can be healed. The answer is that we are already healed. Healing has already been done for us spiritually, but now we need to do something in the natural.

Isaiah 53:5 says, "*But he was wounded for our transgressions, he was bruised for our iniquities: the chastisement of our peace was upon him; and with his stripes we are healed.*" Peter quotes from Isaiah in 1 Peter 2:24 when he says, "*... by whose stripes ye were healed.*"

How Can You Be Healed?

This sermon was preached at Spiritual Hospital in February, 2015.

We can be healed by reverting back to the original environment God created before sin entered the world through obedience and connecting to God. We live in a polluted and fallen world; therefore, we need to use our spiritual weapons.

- Faith: you must receive your healing by faith. And if you have faith as little as a mustard seed...
- Prayer: earthly licence to spiritual interference

- Worship: praising God with singing, dancing, shouting, and clapping of hands.
- Repentance: You can use all the weapons and authority you have been given, but if you don't repent, you won't be healed, because there are still legal grounds for the enemy. You need to repent from your sins and stop from ever doing it again.
- The Word of God: "*He sent his word, and healed them, and delivered them from their destructions,*" (Psalm 107:20). The Word of God is the best medicine available, and it comes with no side effects and is cost efficient.

> *For the word of God is quick, and powerful, and sharper than any two-edged sword, piercing even to the dividing asunder of soul and spirit, and of the joints and marrow, and is a discerner of the thoughts and intents of the heart.*
> —Hebrews 4:12

> *My son, give attention to my words; incline your ear to my sayings. Do not let them depart from your eyes; keep them in the midst of your heart; For they are life to those who find them, and health to all their flesh.*
> —Proverbs 4:20-22

God, and not the method by which you receive healing, is the healer.

- Have someone with the gift of healing pray for you:

> *And these signs will follow those who believe: In My name they will cast out demons; they will speak with new tongues ... they will lay hands on the sick, and they will recover.*
> —Mark 16:17-18, NKJV

> *Is anyone among you sick? Let him call for the elders of the church, and let them pray over him, anointing him with oil in the name of the Lord. And the prayer of faith will save the sick, and the Lord will raise him up. And if he has committed sins, he will be forgiven.*
>
> —James 5:14-15, NKJV

- Use your power and authority: *"Behold, I give unto you power to tread on serpents and scorpions, and over all the power of the enemy: and nothing shall by any means hurt you,"* (Luke 10:19).

How to Access Your Blessing

This sermon was preached at Spiritual Hospital and aired on YES TV in July, 2015.

Let's define blessing. Most people think that a blessing is having a lot of money, a nice car, a big house and property, and other material possessions. All of these things are not real blessings, but the products of a blessing. You can have all these things and still be miserable with no peace, no joy, and no happiness.

A true blessing goes beyond these things. The English Dictionary defines blessings as "something conducive to happiness or welfare." This is accurate, but the true definition of blessings as per the Word of God can be summed up as God's favour and protection. The favour of God is all you need. An education alone won't open doors for you—God is ultimately in control; it doesn't matter whether you're rich or poor, the favour of God will open the door for you. A small portion of God's favour can be worth a year of wages. God's favour will bless you in the mess, in drought, in recession, in global economic crises, and in financial need. He will open doors no one can close. Even with few skills, you will be selected for something good among many qualified colleagues. God's favour will bring restoration of everything the enemy has stolen (Exodus 3:21). God's favour will also:

- produce increased assets (Deuteronomy 33:23)

- win battles you didn't even fight
- bring honour in the midst of adversaries (Exodus 11:3)

Let me inform you that if you have nothing, you are blessed; if you can't buy your next meal, you are blessed; if you have no money in the bank, you are blessed. Regardless of your circumstances, you are blessed. How is that? If you have a million dollars in the bank and are living like a poor man, does that mean you're not a millionaire? It doesn't change the fact. It's only that you are not walking in it. It's the same with your blessings ... you are not walking in them.

God has already established all of your blessings. They are already provided and given to you. Healing was given, wealth was given, joy was given, and peace was given. Unfortunately, they are trapped in the spiritual realm, waiting to be released into the physical. Many people declare a blessing over your life; however, it's not their declaration that counts, but the fact that you are already blessed. God said you are blessed with all spiritual blessing in Christ. Once He makes a decree or sets a law, He cannot go back on it. The problem is you.

How to Keep Your Joy in a Difficult Situation

This sermon was preached at Spiritual Hospital and aired on YES TV in August, 2015.

You might be wondering how you can have joy when you're in a difficult situation, and all you want is some relief. Unfortunately, many people believe that once they receive Christ as their saviour, their troubles and sorrows will disappear ... as if a magic eraser has erased all their negative situations. Please understand that we are still living in a fallen world where everyone is susceptible to disease, hurt, and negative issues. You may be healed from one thing today, but something will happen again. We have an adversary that is like a raging lion, seeking whom he may devour. We are in a spiritual battle, and there are principalities, powers, and rulers of darkness fighting against us every minute. Despite all of this, hold on to the promises of God, and you will find joy.

Deborah Nembhard-Colquhoun

How to Find Joy in Difficult Situations

Renew your mind and emancipate yourself from mental slavery. Your mind determines your attitude, your self-esteem, and your emotions. We need to change our negative thoughts. Emotions are simply data telling us what we have been thinking after something happens to us. We control all of our emotions by what we think. For example, I could be having one of the worst days ever, but as soon as someone tells me about receiving a large sum of money, instantaneously my emotions change. I become very happy, even without seeing the money. Think on things that are lovely, pure, of a good report: *"For as a man thinketh in his heart, so is he,"* (Proverbs 23:7). We must choose where to focus our attention: *"... but this one thing I do, forgetting those things which are behind, and reaching forth unto those things which are before,"* (Philippians 3:13).

We have the ability, according to 2 Corinthians 10:5, to take all of our thoughts (beliefs, imaginations, dreams, and ideas) captive to the obedience of Christ.

How Do You Find Joy in a Time of ...?

Crisis: Encourage yourself in the fact that night does not last forever, but morning eventually arrives. So it will be with your current situation/crisis—it to will also come to an end. Weeping may endure for a night, but joy is coming in the morning (Psalm 30:5).

Persecution: People are persecuting you; they are talking about you, accusing you, and the enemy is against you on every side. But if God is for you, who can be against you? He promised that He would never leave you or forsake you. He will assign angels to encamp around you, to watch and keep you. What the enemy has meant for evil, God will turn around for your good.

A loss: You have lost your job, your business, and your source of income ... or maybe you've lost that thing you love so much, but like He did for Job, God will give you double for your trouble.

Loss of hope: You have missed out on your blessing or on an opportunity, and you feel like all hope is gone—but it's not over until it's over. Not only will God give you another opportunity, He will give you an even better opportunity.

Spiritual Hospital Manual

Your situation is only a test. It will pass. Tell yourself it's going to pass and it's going to be OK. Encourage yourself like David. No one is going to do it for you. Sitting around and feeling sorry won't help you. As a matter a fact, it will bring other problems. Remember that no matter how hard you try, you can't change the past ... but you have the opportunity to make a better future. During troubling times, put on the garment of praise instead of a garment of heaviness/sorrow. As Paul and Silas did during their midnight hour in prison, begin to thank and praise God for what He is going to do. It's amazing what praise does in a situation. Praise will eliminate the spirit of oppression, sadness, and depression. God inhabits the praises of His people. When the pain of your situation intensifies, or when the trouble seems to have come to an end, you know that you're close to your breakthrough, to your blessing.

Turn back the curtain of memory now and then and remember where you were and where you are today. Remember that you have overcome before and you will overcome again. Be aware that the situation you're going through isn't as bad as it appears. Many people would do anything to be in your current situation, because they're sick in a hospital, gasping for their life. All of the money, fame, and education that we worry about are helpless to someone with a terminal sickness.

Connect with the right people. We are relational beings created not to be alone but in relationship. We have the ability to encourage people. Right now you might be thinking: *This is all very good, but you don't understand how I'm feeling in my situation. I feel as if nothing can change or erase it, and nothing can encourage me. You don't know how I feel when my back is against the wall and I feel like is giving up and calling it quits. I've tried drugs, alcohol, and sex to find relief from my situation, but they only bring me temporary satisfaction.* May I ask you if you have tried Jesus? You might say that you have been saved for year and going to church faithfully. You can be baptized, say all the vows, and go to church, but that doesn't mean you had an encounter with Christ. You may not have a personal relationship with Him. You can also be saved but haven't allowed Chris to be the controller of your life.

From personal experience, I can tell you that there is no one that can change a life the way Jesus can change it. He specializes in the impossible. He will take your weeping and your mourning and transform it into joy. He will take out your heart and give you a new one, electrifying it with His power. Jesus will touch your life in a way that no one else can. What you need in difficult times is a supernatural intervention that only God can give.

How Do We Rejoice in Misery?
This sermon was preached at Spiritual Hospital and aired on YES TV in June, 2016.

You need to be born again. You will become a new man. God will give you a new heart and a new mind. He will put His Spirit in you. This is where God works in our life, because we can't do it alone. Even though He's always there, we have moments that require us to call out to Him by prayer and worship. God has placed something in you to withstand all the difficulties of life. He has placed in you the Holy Spirit, but you need to allow Him to comfort you, encourage you, anoint you, and sustain you. He will give you joy that passes all human understanding. You must trust him. Trust in the Lord with all your heart and lean not on your own understanding.

> *Consider it pure joy, my brothers and sisters, whenever you face trials of many kinds, because you know that the testing of your faith produces perseverance. Let perseverance finish its work so that you may be mature and complete, not lacking anything.*
> —James 1:2-4

The Bible says that not only is it possible to find things to be joyful about during trials, but it actually commands us to do so! Job lost his family, his health, his career, and everything he worked towards, but he still found reason to praise God (Job 1:21). Can you imagine losing everything, yet still praising God? There are plenty of other examples throughout the Bible of people who went through awful things that we can't even begin to imagine, but they all still praised God. Their perseverance made their faith stronger.

Christian Joy

Christ is the only source of the Christian's joy. If we are in Christ, we must have joy at all times. Joy should be in our living, in our service, and even in our tribulation. In Philippians 1:21, Paul says, *"For to me to live is Christ ..."* If Christ is in us, we have no choice but to manifest joy, because we're no longer controlled by the sinful nature, but by the Spirit of God. *"Rejoice in the Lord always: and again I say, Rejoice,"* (Philippians 4:4). Once we are in Christ, our aim and purpose is to glorify God in everything we do. We can't truly glorify God without joy. Joy is one of the fruits of the Spirit. In John 15, we're told that in order to produce the fruit of the Spirit, we must abide in the vine, which is Christ Jesus. We abide in Christ by reading the Word of God, spending time with Him in prayer, praising Him, witnessing about Him, doing good works, and fleeing from sin. As we abide in Christ, His life and power flows into us through the Holy Spirit.

Once we are living in the will of God, we will experience great joy, regardless of our circumstances. Once a Christian is rooted in Christ, he or she can rejoice in tribulation, just like the apostle Paul. Paul went through great tribulation but was able to maintain joy. This is because Paul knew in whom he believed and was anchored in Christ completely. It's not easy to rejoice in a gloomy atmosphere, but the joy of the Lord is our strength; in a weary land, the joy of the Lord is a supernatural joy that will change any atmosphere. It doesn't matter the environment we find ourselves in, the joy of the Lord in us should be unchanged.

Jesus came with joy not to be served, but to serve. We are also to follow in His footsteps. We're not to serve with complaints or grouchiness. It's impossible to do a good service if we're not joyful. God has given us joy so that we can be at peace with ourselves and extend it to others in whatever service we might render. The joy of the Spirit is not a fruit to be kept hidden or allowed to rot, but it's to be displayed and shared. Our service to God and to others should be joyful; otherwise, it won't be effective. God loves a cheerful server. We'll find fulfillment in joyful service, and we'll receive eternal rewards from God. God will not accept dead sacrifices; therefore, we must go before Him with a joyful heart. We miss out on all our benefits when our offerings are not accepted ... but when our offerings are accepted, all the treasures of Heaven are open to us.

Renewing your Mind

This sermon was preached at Spiritual Hospital and aired on YES TV in September, 2015.

It's important to renew your mind so that you can walk in peace, joy, and happiness, fulfilling your destiny and achieving all that God intended for you. You will see life more positively. Your mind has control over every action you take. It controls your thoughts, and it tells your body exactly what to do in any given situation. It tells your mouth what to speak and what to eat. It tells your eyes what to look at and your ears what to listen to and what to tune out. It tells your brain what to think about; it tells your entire being how to respond in every single situation. Your mind is the foundation of your intellect, which controls your personal self-esteem and drives you to succeed.

Your mind can also be influenced by the enemy. It's where the enemy launches most of his attacks, which leads to inconsistency and depression. In this state, you can't love the Lord with all your heart, strength, soul and mind. This is why Paul says "... *but be ye transformed by the renewing of your mind*," (Romans 12:2).

Understanding the Human Mind

The human mind is a highly organized, complex, and integrated processing information system that governs everything you do. It has over a million sensory receptors. Your mind determines your attitude, your self-esteem, and your emotions. It's like a computer hard-drive in which there are more megabits than you realize. Your entire life's worth of information is programmed in your mind. Your experiences, habits, skills, and visual images are filed in your mind.

Let's Analyze Your Mind

Your conscious mind uses about 11 per cent of the brain's capacity. You have full control over the conscious mind, where you're able to analyze, solve problems, and make decisions. Your subconscious mind uses about 89 per cent of your brain's capabilities. It's similar to a huge filing cabinet containing endless information. Unlike the conscious mind, the subconscious mind isn't under your control. You're driven by the subconscious mind, which is why you develop habits and you do things without being aware of them. Your subconscious mind is where you find your identity, values, beliefs, habits, emotions, and self-control. Your conscious mind retrieves things from your sub-conscious mind; however, even if all the things that are stored in the subconscious mind are true, you have the ability in the conscious mind not to believe them.

Negative Effect of the Mind

The negative beliefs you have in your mind can kill you. Do you know that you can be healed and still believe in your mind that you're sick? We can pray all we want, but you will still be sick.

Freedom begins in the mind. You can be free physically but not mentally. You have been set free from bondage, but you're still trapped in mental slavery. As a result, you're living a defeated life.

Examples of Negative Thoughts

- There is poverty in your generational lineage, so you tell yourself that you will be poor.
- You grew up in the projects and still drop into the projects, even if there are many doors open for you.
- You're not happy in your relationship because your partner has not met your expectation.

If there's no "mind" change, there will never be any "life" change.

There are ways to reprogram the subconscious mind to remove negativity. Limited beliefs and negative habits can be reprogrammed by using declarations. The subconscious mind learns through repetition. Every belief and habit you possess was formed through repetition; we can implant new ones the same way. Declarations are an effective way to plant positive messages into your subconscious. It's one of the most effective ways to change a limited or negative belief. If you continuously say "this is never going to work," then it's highly probable that things never will.

Studies have shown that patterns in our brain can be rewired through cognitive behavioural therapy or affirmations. Declarations change the way our brains are wired. Repetition of a declaration changes the neural pathways in your brain over time to produce the new belief.

The Bible says that if we decree a thing, it must come to pass. You must replace your negative identity through repetition. Here are some positive declarations that you can use to reprogram your mind:

- I am who God says I am; I can do what God says I can do. I am the head and not the tail.
- God has given me power to obtain wealth. I am brilliant and can use my mind, talents, gifts, and abilities to produce wealth.
- I am destined to greatness. I will live a life of divine purpose.
- I am spiritually, emotionally, financially, mentally, and psychologically sound.
- I am wealthy and money flows to me.
- I am fearfully and wonderfully made by God. My birth is not an accident. I wasn't born just to add to the earth's population. I have a divine purpose, a divine mandate.
- The Word of God says that I am a royal priest and a peculiar person. I was born to fill a gap.

This is why as a student in school we are told to study using repetition. We are also told to study the Word of God.

Spiritual Hospital Manual

Meditation/ Dreams
The Word of the Lord says, "*This book of the law should not depart out of they mouth; but thou shalt meditate therein day and night,*" (Joshua 1:8). Even natural words have power. Not only will your mind be settled and focused, but you'll be able to resist negative thoughts. When you meditate, the mind takes pictures and records them in your subconscious mind. The more you meditate on something, the more it lodges deep inside of you.

Meditating on the Word of God will also help to delete the negative words in your mind and replace them with positive words. That is why the Word of God tells us to think on things that are lovely, pure, and of a good report. Many successful people dream or visualize about their great achievements before they become a reality. Bill Gates must have dreamt about computer software before it became a reality. "*For as he thinketh in his heart, so is he,*" (Proverbs 23:7).

Dr. Walter Staples said:

Therefore be very careful about what you allow to control your mind and what you think about. What you think about surely becomes your character and identity. No matter how poor your background was, whether you were neglected or are down trodden, you have what it takes to be at the top.

The key to success lies in your particular manner of thinking. When you change how you think about yourself, your relationships, your goals, and your world, your life changes. If you change the quality of your thinking, you necessarily will change the quality of your life.[1]

Talking to Yourself in a Positive Way
We've all heard the words, "people who talk to themselves are losing it." This is society's way of dealing with something they don't care to understand. The statement, in fact, is not true. Every single person at some time or another will talk to themselves. Some people are just not aware

---

[1] "Renew Your Mind: Don't Dwell on the Past," Modern Ghana, accessed September 26, 2016, https://www.modernghana.com/news/511225/renew-your-mind-dont-dwell-on-the-past.html.

that they're having a conversation in their mind. If you've ever thought *I cannot do that*, or *Where am I?* and responded to those thoughts, then you've had a conversation in your mind.

I want you to be aware that you are actually speaking to yourself, and I encourage you to be mindful and speak positive things. Believe it or not, you can also program things in your mind by talking to yourself.

Think that you are strong. Repeat this thought over and over again so that your mind doesn't program the bad thought, but rather the positive one. Dismiss the negative thought immediately before it can surface. Don't feed it and don't hesitate to dismiss it immediately.

Your subconscious mind will believe whatever you tell it the most; therefore, you must spend time each day deliberately speaking positive things to yourself. It's only through repetition that your subconscious mind will adopt its new programming. Only then will you begin to change the engine of your mind to think these new thoughts automatically.

Change Your Worldly Thinking
If you've thought of something negative, even if it's true, never think about it again. Override those thoughts with something opposite. You control all of your emotions by what you think. I could be having one of the worst days ever, but as soon as I hear that I'm going to receive something good, instantaneously my emotions change. I become very happy (even without seeing the thing). It's important to guard our thought life. Isaiah 26:3 tells us that if we keep our minds focused on God, He will keep us in perfect peace.

Remove yourself from toxic people and connect yourself with influential people who will speak life into you. Words are like seeds; you plant them and they start to grow. Uproot old, negative words and replant new, positive words. Some of the things that have been sown into your life are like an old oak tree. First the seed was planted, and then the tree became bigger and bigger, stronger and stronger. The roots grew so deep into the ground that it's almost impossible to root them up. This is where the supernatural God comes in.

God's Word
Our mind is programmed to think from a worldly perspective—the lust of the eyes, the lust of the flesh, and the pride of life. The only way to fix the error of the world's thinking is to replace it with God's truth, and the only infallible source of God's truth is found in His revealed Word, the Bible.

Being Born Again
As Christians, we are to occupy the mind with/as Christ: "*Let this mind be in you, which was also in Christ Jesus,*" (Philippians 2:5). We must set our affections on things above (Colossians 3:2). We must strive to become Christ-like by walking in love and obedience, just as Jesus did. We must also have a renewed mind (Romans 12:2).

Utilize Your Power over Your Thoughts
Take every one of your thoughts (beliefs, imaginations, dreams, and ideas) captive to the obedience of Christ. (2 Corinthians 10:5).

The Holy Spirit
"*The god of this world* [Satan] *has blinded the minds of the unbelieving, so that they might not see the light of the gospel of the glory of Christ,*" (2 Corinthians 4:4).

The Holy Spirit will regenerate and transform our minds if we allow Him. Not only can God delete the negative thoughts so you won't remember them anymore, but He will dismantle their effect. You'll still see them, but through the eyes of the Holy Spirit. The bad things someone did to you are in your imagination, but instead of seeing them as wicked, you now see the enemy behind them and love them instead.

With the supernatural ability of the Holy Spirit, you are able to judge, discern, and pick up things that the natural eye (natural mind) would never be able to see or understand. We are given supernatural wisdom and ability to discern the true situation and see everything that happens to us from God's vantage point.

Having a renewed mind, putting off our own negative thoughts, and putting on the mind of Christ is the only way we can begin to see everything that happens to us from God's perspective and not get buried by our own thoughts.

The Mind Is Spiritual
Did you know that the brain is not natural? You're able to see it in the natural and comprehend it to a degree, but the source and generator of the human brain is spiritual. If a human brain malfunctions, the only way to fix it correctly is through the spiritual. Doctors and medication can only temporally solve an issue of the human brain. It would be similar to putting a bandage on a cut that requires stitches. Nobody on Earth can create or transplant a brain. Once a person is dead, they're dead. The only one who can fix the human brain is the one who created it. Not only is He able to fix it, but He is the only one who can replace it.

All hospitals are run by an authority figure. I believe that it's appropriate that I introduce you to ours. Not only is He the authoritative figure, but He is the CEO, director, and controller. Can I introduce you to Him? He is the great physician and the mighty God; He rules eternity. His name is Jesus. He is the Kings of kings, the Lord of lords. Demons tremble at the very mention of His name. Every knee shall bow and every tongue shall confess the Jesus Christ is Lord.

A Synopsis of God's Sovereignty
Who is God?
Do you know God? I've come to realize that many people, including Christians, know about God, but don't really know Him.

Omnipresence
God is everywhere at the same time. He fills every dimension, scope, and galaxy. He inhabits the heavens, earth, sea, and under the sea. He's in the physical and the spiritual. He can be with everyone in the world at the same time. This is why David says in Psalms 139:8 that he can't flee from God's presence. You can't run from God. Jonah tried to run from God, and ended up in the belly of a fish. God is even in the belly of a fish.

There is no secret you can hide from Him. Everything is naked and fully exposed to Him, even your deepest thoughts. Everyone can be thinking and talking at the same time, and He is able to hear each one distinctively. What kind of God is this God? He is the all-knowing God.

Omniscient
Omniscient means having an infinite awareness, understanding, and insight. It's complete knowledge. God knows your past, your present, and your future. He knows those that are wrongly accusing you, your ups and downs, your going out and coming in; He is so accurate that He knows every strand of hair on your head.

Satan will whisper to your mind and tell you that God doesn't care, but don't believe the lie of the enemy. God knows what you are going through every day. Everything about God is love; He is all love— His attributes, the core aspect of His character. He is unconditional, agape love.

You may think that even though He is all knowing, all present, and all loving, He can't help you. Let me inform you that He is also Omni-competent. He is able to handle any situation, having the authority and legal capacity to act in all matters.

Omnipotent
God is omnipotent, which means He has unlimited authority or influence; He is a force of unlimited power. God is the source of all power in Heaven and on Earth. There is no other force that exists to challenge His deity. He is in control of the entire universe ... past, present, and future. God is the final judge who overrides governments, kings, rulers, and judges. That's why we often refer to Him as Lord of lords and King of kings.

He is Omnificent—Unlimited in Creative Power
Everything that exists is a product made by God. Doctors and scientists are limited and depend on the creation of God to operate. Do you know why they're not able to breathe breath into man? Because they are limited. God has the blueprint and will never share it with man.

Whenever I think of the human body and all of its intricate details, like lungs that pump air, blood that flows with oxygen and regenerates the body, or a heart that pumps blood, I realize that God is awesome. The brain is so complex; only a sovereign God could create and sustain such a masterpiece.

Who is God?

God is mighty. He is a deliverer, a healer, a way maker, a counsellor, and a friend. He is your advocate and strong tower. He is the way, the truth, and the life. God specializes in taking the mess you made and turning it into a great message of restoration. God will wipe your bad track record absolutely clean and take your sins and throw them into the sea of forgetfulness where He will remember them no more.

The Voice of God

All of God's children have the ability to hear God's voice, but many of us are not listening. Jesus says in John 10:27 that *"My sheep hear my voice, and I know them, and they follow me ..."* After reading this section, you will know how to hear God's voice. Hearing God's voice makes a big difference. The Word from God is going to sustain you in the good and bad times. It will be there in the test, the fire, and the storm. His Word will comfort you when everyone is laughing at you, mocking you, or telling you to give up. God spoke to Noah five different times, and to Sarah and Abraham eight times. The voice of God will give you victory and health and guide you from destruction, leading you into blessings, peace, joy, and contentment.

How to Hear the Voice of God

- By listening: Block out the noise. Like Jesus did when praying, we can retreat to a solitary place.
- By seeking God: If you seek Him, you shall find Him.
- By having faith that God will speak: Everything in the Kingdom of God operates by faith.

Spiritual Hospital Manual

- By tuning into the channel of Heaven: How do you tune in to the right channel to hear God's voice? Just like with a radio, you need the right frequency. Sin, the enemy's voice, your own voice, the voice of other people, are all noises that can affect the frequency.
- By being in God's presence: We will hear through our spiritual ears. We can tap into Heaven's frequency through praise and worship, where our spiritual antenna will signal Heaven. We can tune into the frequency by focusing on and thinking about the things of Heaven.
- By praying: Prayer is communion with God, but often we have a one-way conversation. You cannot have a relationship with God and be the only person talking. Take the time to stop and wait upon the Lord. He will speak to you.
- By obeying God: Disobeying God is the foundation of sin, and sin separates us from God. Sin is like fog or a steel wall.
- By identifying how God speaks: God speaks through different means, even through the mouth of donkey

How Does God speak?
God uses different channels of communication to speak to us.

- People, preachers, TV, and other media: How do you know that the person giving the message is sent from God? You can look at a person's walk with God to see if he/she is sent from God. You can be sure that God isn't going to use just anyone to be His messenger. He will use faithful servants who love Him, who do His will, and who are courageous. God will use a pastor's sermon to speak to you directly about a particular situation, or to answer a question that you've been asking Him through prayer.
- Circumstances and troubles: He will take your support system away from you so that you'll know that He was with

you all along. Most people come to God through trouble. If some of us don't have trouble, we won't need God.
- Prophecy or a word of knowledge
- Our thoughts and the still small voice: There are two voices that speak into your thoughts and can affect your ability to hear God's voice. They are your own voice and the voice of Satan through demonic prompting. How do you differentiate between the two voices? Satan's voice usually increases negative emotions and makes you feel upset, angry, fearful, ashamed, condemned, and guilty. He'll tell you to go out and kill someone or to hate yourself. He'll convince you that everything is over and there is no hope. The enemy's voice comes with confusion. Our own voice is usually very analytical or logical. God's voice can be distinguished because it will line up with the Bible and His character. There is peace, joy, and love in God's voice. God will often speak to you through the small still voice of His Holy Spirit. After you have been saved, God may speak to you a lot through a small still voice. He will tell you to pray or to do something specific.
- The inner heart, the heart of the soul: This voice is like a navigator, a GPS system, that will navigate you through life. A GPS system will tell you to turn onto Lawrence Avenue, but it doesn't tell you that you are going to go past a McDonald's and a Shell gas station. God doesn't always give you the details, either. He will tell you ADZ, but not necessarily ABC. This is because God operates by faith, and He wants you to walk by faith and not by sight.
- You heart, through impressions: God will impress upon your heart, prompting you to give someone some food or money, or to call someone who is in trouble. He transfers His thoughts into you, and suddenly someone may come to your mind, or shortly afterwards call you or appear in the room. Sometimes an idea forms in your mind that seems to pop up from nowhere. Some people pursue

the idea and become millionaires. Please note that when God gives you an idea, it's inspirational. When the devil gives you an idea, it's temptation.
- Signs around us: God says we will know that His coming is near by the signs around us. If the trees are putting forth buds, you know that spring is near. Your car engine light will speak to you, telling you something is wrong with the car engine. God will speak to you in the same way.
- His Spirit: God spoke to the men of old audibly, but today He speaks to us through His Spirit. When He speaks in your spirit, you will usually get a feeling of a quickening or a flooding. The Holy Spirit in you confirms that it is truly God. You just know that you know it is God. Sometimes you find yourself moving out and doing things, and afterwards you wonder how you were able to accomplish the task. The Holy Spirit was speaking to your spirit, and you operated in obedience to the voice without even realizing it.
- His Word: God spoke to individuals in the days of the Old Testament, including Adam, Eve, Abraham, and Noah. He is speaking today. He is the same yesterday, today, and forever. The Bible states that God speaks. He designed His Word to speak to us as we read. The Bible is the only book that is fully alive. As you read the Bible, words will jump off the pages and come alive to you. This is why you can read the same verse or passage of scripture over and over again and get different insights each time. All you need to do is move out in obedience. For example, you don't need to ask God to save you, because He told you how to be saved. You don't have to ask God if He wants you to forgive someone, because He said to forgive. You may want to know what God thinks about you. It's all in Scripture. You don't have to hear the plan God has for you over and over again, because He has already spoken that the plans He has for you are all good.

- Dreams and visions: God can speak to you through a dream while you're sleeping or a vision while you're awake. God uses this method in the Muslim world. Many Muslims who have never read the Word of God are coming to Christ through dreams and visions. How can you know if your dream or vision is from God? The Holy Spirit that lives inside of you will bear witness that the dream or vision you're having is from God.
- Writing: As I'm writing things pertaining to God, He speaks to me. I am getting insights, revelation, and understanding. This is not me, but God speaking to me.

God spoke to Abraham and told him to take his son, Isaac, to the land of Moriah and offer him as a burnt offering. Now when the time came for the sacrifice, Abraham took out his knife and was going to kill Isaac, but God told Abraham not to lay his hand on his son or do anything to him. God was testing Abraham to see if he feared Him.

I have come too far by faith. The blessings of God are too close for me to give up now. Destiny is calling me. Divine favour will not pass me by. I am going to hold on to the voice of God.

Mini Sermon
"If God be for us, who can be against us?" (Romans 8:31).

My message today will be taken from Romans 8:31. My topic today is "If God is for us, who can be against us?" Paul is speaking specifically to the persecuted Christians during the Roman times. This text is meant to be understood in the context of the chapter, but I'm going to relate it to us in this time.

I'm going to relate it to the Body of Christ. I'm ministering to Christians today, but if there is someone here who isn't saved, you will make Jesus your Lord and Saviour. When you do this, there is assurance that He will be for you, and nobody can be against you. What an assurance for the believers! Sometimes we don't take note of what the Scriptures say. This passage is so encouraging to us when we are going through situations.

Paul is asking a rhetorical question to get his students to think. He's trying to make a point, because in the previous verses he established that because of our sanctification, our justification, our glorification, and our security in Christ, nobody can be against us. You have to grasp the scripture, because it's an encouragement in times of trouble.

Please note that Paul isn't saying that you won't have any enemies. He's not saying that you won't go through testing or persecution and trials. He's saying that our enemy, Satan, will not be successful against us. He goes on to say that all things work together for good for those that love God and are called by His purpose. The enemy is trying to pursue us, but he will not be victorious against us. If God is for us, who really will be truly against us? Nothing and no one! Not even the highest rank of demons, rulers, and principalities can be against us. We need to know this, because if we don't, we'll be discouraged and give up. But my confidence and re-assurance today is that if God is for me, nothing can be against me.

We bless God! In accordance with God's good purpose, nothing can happen to you once you are a child of God, walking in obedience to Him. I'll go back to even Job in the Scriptures. For those who know Job quite well, Job was going through a time of persecution, but even though the enemy was doing all these things to him, the enemy could not have touched him unless he got permission or approval from God. Nothing can happen to you unless God gives approval. Sometimes we wonder why things happen to us, and sometimes we won't know until we leave this earth, but we can be sure that if God is for us, nothing can be against us!

Some of the things we go through are to try us and prove us and to build our faith. It can be tough, but there is a plan and a purpose through it all. We glorify the Lord. It's our confidence in God that even during times of persecution, nothing can happen, because God is for us.

As I mention earlier, I'm going to relate our text to us today as Christians. Paul was referring to the persecuted Christians. How many of you are going through persecution? How many of you are going through testing and trials? Let me encourage you this morning if you're going through a situation in which it seems like everybody and everyone is against you. Glory to God! Everybody and everyone is against you; it feels like every time you put one foot forward, something is pulling you back. You cannot progress forward. Am I speaking to someone this morning? It feels like every time you put one foot forward, something is pulling you back.

Can I encourage you that maybe it's God pulling you back? Maybe God is allowing the enemy to pull you back so that you'll not end up in a trap. I'm here to tell you that you may feel pulled back, but God is going to take you out of your situation sooner or later. He is going to pull you forward. The Bible says that the steps of the righteous man are ordered by God. God is going to order your steps into greatness, and you're going to see in the spiritual realm that there is more for you than those that are against you.

You may feel like you're trapped in a fire that is intensifying. I can just visualize the fourth man in your fire situation, and that fourth man is Jesus. He's going to take you out of your fire. Perhaps you feel like you're in a raging storm; the wind and the waves won't calm down, but I'm here to let you know this morning that even the wind and the waves obey God. Jesus was in a storm when He was on Earth, and He spoke to that storm, and the wind and the waves obeyed Him. It was a physical wind and a physical storm, but even the spiritual wind and the spiritual storm that you are going through can be calmed. I know of somebody who can calm the storm for you. As a matter of fact, He is on the case, and somebody's storm is about to cease. God is going to cease the storm for you if you believe and receive it! Right now He is speaking to someone's storm, and I'm here to tell you that you are coming out of your storm. You are coming out of that wind, because God almighty is going to take you out of it. The storm was not sent to kill you or consume you, but you are going to learn something from that storm. You are going to see the hands of God, the might of God, and the power of God. Alleluia! Thank you, Jesus.

There is a Red Sea before you, but I'm here to let you know that God can part that Red Sea for you. He specializes in things that are impossible, and there is nothing that He cannot do Glory to God! Oh,

Jesus! Sickness is against you, but the Bible tells me that He was wounded for your transgressions. He was bruised for your iniquity, and by His stripes, you are healed. You are healed! Glory to God! He is coming through for somebody. Many want to bring accusations against you.

I'm touching different situations, because your situation, Minister Diane or Pastor David, is not my situation. Everybody is going through some kind of situation, and the enemy wants to bring accusation against you. He wants to accuse you of your past. The enemy is bringing it up to you and lying to you, and you cannot move forward because all you can think of is what you did back then. Ah Jesus! But verse thirty-three of the scripture we just read says that nobody can bring charges against God's elect, because God is the one that justifies. He died for us while we were yet sinners. He died in your place. It was paid in full; it was finished. We sinned and messed up, but we can get back up again and God's mercy will be able to forgive us.

Jesus is the light of your salvation; the Lord is the strength of your life, so of whom should you be afraid? The wicked may seem to be against you, but God is on your side. I am preaching, but sometimes people don't grasp that God is truly on their side. I am confident that He is on my side. I am not talking about any little god. I am talking about the King of the universe. I am talking about the "I am that I am." I am talking about the sustainer God.

As Pastor mentioned this morning, He is the one who put a liver into you and created a bladder. Who can create a human being with such intricate detail? Only God can do it, and if that awesome God is for you, who else can be against you? He is on your side this morning. We need to learn to trust Him and depend on Him through the storms, through the trials, and through the testing. Maybe you can't see a way out or imagine how He's going to take you out, but if you take a moment to meditate and think about who God is, you'll be reassured that there is a God of grace, compassion, and love. He will find a way for you to escape, but you need to trust Him.

The Bible says not to depend on your own understanding. I am encouraging somebody this morning to lean not into your own understanding, but in all of your ways acknowledge the almighty God, and He will direct your paths. Not only will He direct your path, but He'll take you out of your trials. Weeping may endure for one night, but joy is coming in the morning. God will not sit back and watch the enemy destroy you. God will not sit back and watch the enemy wins. He is too loving.

You may be wondering why you're going through the testing, and why it's taking so long. One of the reasons you may be struggling is that you're not reading the Word of God and listening to what He's saying to you. Perhaps you're not walking in obedience. I'm not talking about everybody here. Maybe you've been struggling for so long because you refuse to utilize the weapons that God has given to you. Maybe you're not truly saved. You may believe you are saved because you go to church every day, pay your tithes, and was baptized. You may have even said the sinner's prayer, but just because you wanted what God could give you rather than what you could give to God. You may do all this, but is your heart right with God? When you made your vow, did you give God your whole being? Did you surrender your heart to Him?

Salvation is not about repeating words after the priest, or some sort of ritual. It's a personal relationship with God. Is Jesus your Lord and Saviour? Oh Glory to God! I am speaking to somebody this morning ... somebody who thinks they're serving God, but all Hell is around them because they don't have a covering. God is not in their life. God is around their life, and He's knocking on the door of their heart, but He has not come in yet. When He comes to your heart, make Him your Lord. Even through the tests and the trials and pain, you will still trust Him.

Many people are cursing God and asking why He allows trials. This message may seem and look simple, but once we believe and are part of God, He will contend for us. He will come through for you. Many of you are going through a test, and you're holding on and saying, "I am trusting the Lord." Keep trusting Him! You're not missing out anything, because God will restore it a hundredfold. He will give you double for your trouble, like He did for Job.

God will never fail you. He has never failed me yet, and I've gone through the fire; I've gone through the flood. I've gone through testing and trials, but God took me out. He took me out so that I can encourage you this morning that daylight is coming for you. Daylight is coming for somebody. Please don't just go home and let it be another message. We all go through something, but once we hold onto God, we hold onto Jesus. He will come through. He will find a way when there seems to be no way.

We focus so much on the temporal, but we need to take our sights to greater heights. We're all on a journey and passing through this land, but our hope is up there. We become discouraged when we focus on our material things, but we should put our eyes on Jesus. Soon we are going to leave this Earth. The Bible tells us that the signs of the times are everywhere. Hypocrites cannot discern the signs. Our works and efforts should be directed at eternity.

We all live in a fallen, messed up world. Mankind, not God, is to blame for this, because we fell from grace. We disobeyed God and didn't listen to His instructions. We have a part of Adam in us, but the grace of God, the love of God, restores us. What does it profit anyone to gain this whole world but lose their soul? Be encouraged this morning that God is on your side, and be encouraged that you will be leaving this Earth very soon. There is a mansion in Heaven waiting for you. The Bible tells me that there will be no more pain, no more suffering, and no more sorrow. My God! Can you imagine? Can you imagine that there is a hope for the believers? Glory to God! We will all celebrate. Oh Glory to God! He is preparing a place for us.

Your Today Is Going to Change Tomorrow
Your tomorrow may not be a literal tomorrow; it's a figure of speech. Your tomorrow could be tomorrow, but it could also be next week, next month, or next year.

Today represents the negative things you are going through—the pain, the suffering, the heartache, the trials, or the testing ... whether they are a result of your past, your generation, or your own decisions, curses, or spells.

Many of you are about to throw in the towel. Nothing seems to be worth it anymore. You feel as if life has no more meaning; you might as well call it quits. I am here to prophecy that you are coming out of your situation. I am here to decree and declare that you are coming out today. You are at an intersection in your life; you are at a transition point in your life. You are about to cross over to the next day; morning is just behind your dark clouds. You are about to come out of Egypt, out of bondage and oppression, and cross over to the land of Canaan to your promised land. You can't give up now. Your breakthrough is just daylight away. You have gone through too much to give up now; you have suffered too much to lose. You can't afford to give up now.

You wouldn't feel the way you're feeling if you could only get a glimpse of your future. Many times people have missed their very best blessing because they give up too soon. Do you know that when it seems as though the fire has turned up, that's a sign that you are close to your breakthrough, your victory?

Storms don't last forever. The night doesn't last forever. There must be daylight. The sun is going to shine. Scientists can't stop the sun from shining; no power on Earth can stop the sun from shining or cause the storm to stop, but I know someone who can. He can stop and control both the physical sun and the spiritual sun. He speaks to the wind, and it obeys Him.

How Is Your Today Going to Change Tomorrow?

Don't let depression take a hold of your life and make you feel like a hostage. Your situation was meant to change. God has not ordained that any night should endure forever, or that any storm should last forever. You may feel as if the fire will last for a long time, but be assured that Jesus is in the fire with you, and He will carry you through it. God is a faithful God and will reward those who are diligently seeking after Him. Weeping may endure for a night, but joy is coming in the morning.

We weren't originally created to suffer hardships. It was not part of God's plan for our lives; however, when Adam and Eve sinned against God through disobedience, the world came under a curse. It's because of this curse that we face trials and tribulation. Many Christians suffer lengthy battles, and some even perish because of their situation, due to their lack knowledge about how to escape. God spoke in His Word: "*Beloved, I wish above all things that thou mayest prosper and be in good health, even as thy soul prospeth,*" (3 John 2); "*Every good gift and every perfect gift is from above, and cometh down from the Father of Lights, with whom is no variableness, neither shadow of turning,"* (James 1:17); *"I am come that they might have life, and that they might have it more abundantly,"* (John 10:10).

Joy is in that life, peace is in that life, health is in that life, and prosperity is in that life. Sin has robbed you of this life, but God has provided restoration. All we have to do is take authority, use our power, and close the legal ground you give the enemy through sin, disobedience, unforgiveness, and bitterness.

Most of your blessings and your breakthroughs only happen when you are in God's will. We call these conditional blessings. Being a Christian is the main prerequisite, but you don't have to be a Christian for some things to change in your life. Some blessings are just general and will happen despite your current situation. God will rain on the just and the unjust. Some people are walking around as though they deserve the good life they are living. God is also a covenant keeper. He made covenant to our generation in the Old Testament, stating that He would bless our seed and that we would be a product of that blessing. Some people are reaping what their great grandparents sowed. God has also blessed some people for His own purposes, and others so that they can be a blessing.

Don't let your current situation discourage you. Bill Gates was just an ordinary man, but one day he became one of the richest men on Earth. Many on the TV show *American Idol* started out as ordinary people, but now they are superstars. Ordinary people can have nothing one day and wake up the next day completely changed because they won the lottery.

You might just be an ordinary person today, but it takes just takes a few seconds for your destiny to change through the grace of God. For those who are saved, you have God's favour upon your life just waiting to happen, and His favour goes beyond fame, education, wisdom, connections, or laws. God's favour supersedes anything. When it comes to you, the sky has no limit. He will open doors that no one can close. He will cause people out of nowhere to bless you; He connects you with people in high places.

In the Bible, we read that Joseph's brothers threw him into a pit and sold him into slavery, which eventually led to him being put into prison. God's favour was upon his life as Joseph went through all of his tribulations, and he eventually became the prime minister.

You might be in a global crisis, but God will favour you. Jacob was in a global crisis, yet God's favour overtook him. When everyone else was suffering through a famine, Jacob became a billionaire because he was blessed. We are blessed and will find favour with God.

The God of the impossible will make a way of escape for you. He is the only one that can make something out of nothing. You might miss your reaping season because you have fallen, or someone has put a spell on you, but God controls the seasons and is going to bring your reaping season back around. If God is for you, who can be against you? It might not look good right now, but that doesn't change the fact that you are blessed.

God is working behind the scenes, arranging things in your favour. He is making a way where you don't see a way; therefore, you don't have to live a worried, stressed-out life trying to force everything to happen. All you need to do is keep God first in your heart. You're not here by accident. You have been chosen by the Creator of the universe for a specific plan in your life, something for you to accomplish.

The enemy doesn't fight you for where you are now; he fights you for where you're going. You may be facing difficulty, but it's only because God has something amazing in your future. There are new levels of your destiny; you haven't touched the surface of what God has in store. You're going to see Ephesians 3:20 come to pass. God is able to do exceedingly abundantly above all that we can ever ask or think. What is meant for your harm, God said He would use to your advantage. When you can't see a way, God can make a way. When it looks like it's over, God has the final say.

God Uses Ordinary People to Do Extraordinary Things

I want to talk to you today about how God works in ordinary people, because if you don't understand this, you could miss your blessing. You may become depressed and miss how God works in Spiritual Hospital.

You could end up trapped in your mediocre state, or block others' progress and blessings. It's time we get out of ourselves, because there is a dying world out there depending upon you and me.

How does society define "ordinary?" With words such as simple, normal, plain, and regular. Ordinary means to be undistinguished, with no special features; somewhat inferior or below average. It can also be defined as weak, powerless, poor, illiterate, ugly, and unskilled.

Society defines what an ordinary person is based on the fact that they are limited to the natural. They cannot discern how God works. When someone is not saved, the Hoy Spirit of God is not living in them (1 Corinthians 2; Ephesians 1:9-19). Without the Holy Spirit in them, they cannot discern the deep things of God. This should not be the case with the Christians, although some spiritually immature Christians can't see God working in ordinary things.

To know and understand how God works, you have to know Him. Do you know Him, or do you only know about Him? Going to church, being baptized, and even accepting God as your Lord and Saviour doesn't constitute knowing God. You could watch all the news about the Queen, read all the books about her, learn about her favorite pet, and even her birth date, but that doesn't mean that you know her. Why? Because you've never met her. You've never talked to her. You've never had any kind of personal interaction or relationship with her at all. Sadly, this is the same with most Christians. They hear about God, hear all about the mighty works He does, but they've never experienced Him first-hand; they have no relationship with Him.

There's a test you can do to find out if you really do know Him. You can find it in 1 John 2:3-4. You can tell that you really know God if you obey Him. This verse explains that whoever claims to know Him, but doesn't do what He commands, is a liar, and the truth is not in that person.

How does God work in ordinary people? God works in the ordinary by doing things that most people may not notice. God chose the foolish things of the world to shame the wise; God chose the weak things of the world to shame the strong. He chose the lowly things of this world and the despised things—and the things that are not—to nullify the things that are, so that no one may boast before Him. He specializes in the impossible. He is the source of everything. He is all powerful and sovereign. He will take your nothing and make it into something. He works in individuals by His Spirit. He'll take their lack, their nothing, and place His power in them. He will supernaturally transfer His power to you to heal, deliver, and set the captive free. He also works through His divine Word. The Word of God is quick, active, and sharper than any two-edged sword. His Word is one of the most powerful weapons on Earth. More dangerous that any nuclear bomb. The Lord can take men and women from the humblest of circumstances, put His power in them, and make them able of mighty exhibitions of the Spirit and power.

Why does God do this? So that His glory will show and no one will take the glory. God doesn't need any of our natural wisdom or our influential positions to accomplish His work. He is God all by Himself. When God mightily uses what the world arrogantly calls stupid, weak, poor, or despised people, then God alone will receive the glory, and not man.

God Uses Ordinary People in the Bible
Peter and John were unschooled, ordinary men, yet they healed many. Peter was a fisherman, but when his shadow fell on some people as he passed by, they were healed. Crowds gathered from the towns around Jerusalem, bringing their sick and those tormented by evil spirits, and all of them were healed. The Jewish priests, scribes, and elders suffered from superiority, believing that only a limited number of people in high positions could be used by the Lord.

Matthew was a tax collector. His occupation was a despised one in Israel, yet this despised tax collector became one of the original twelve apostles and the author of Matthew's Gospel. Peter, James, John, and Andrew? They were plain old fishermen, but God choose them to lay the foundation for His church.

We expect ministers of the Gospel to do extraordinary ministry, but simple Christians to remain ordinary. Ananias was a simply devout, respected disciple of the Lord (Acts 9:10; 22:12); nevertheless, he was used by God to heal a renowned apostle's blindness.

God uses "ignorant" people to do His work on Earth. Moses came from tending sheep in the desert to leading Israel out of Egypt. Daniel came out of slavery and captivity in Babylon to become the godly assistant to the King of Babylon.

You might think that these men and the Apostle Paul were well educated, but education can't cast out demons, heal sicknesses and diseases, or discern the thoughts of man to save.

Jesus Christ came to this Earth, not as flamboyant royalty (the "world's" way), but as an obscure baby, born in a stable, who grew up in a humble part of Israel and worked as a carpenter. It wasn't by accident that the Son of God did this, thereby forever demonstrating to us the humility that God requires of His people.

Billy Graham is just another ordinary guy. God has used him in an extraordinary way, reaching thousands, even millions, of people with the Gospel.

Despite the many struggles I had accepting my place in ministry, I have come to accept that God has chosen me. I'm not very intellectual, well spoken, or fit for the role ... according to society. I can't dot all my I's or cross all my T's, but I've come to realize that I am not man's choice, but that God has chosen me. God uses the foolish things of the world to confound the wise. Whatever I do, to God be all the glory. David was not the chosen one according to his siblings or others. How could a little shepherd boy be a king? Man looks at the outward, but God sees the heart. David was the apple of God's eye. God's choice isn't based on your looks, your education, your intellect, your wealth, or even your seniority.

You can't figure out God. You can't comprehend Him. He takes a nobody and turns them into a somebody, the reject into the acceptable, the poor into the rich. He takes the scum and cleans them up.

What Is Your Position Today?

- Change the way you view others and yourself.

- Samson was a womanizer.
- David was a murderer who had an affair.
- Noah was a drunkard.
- Moses had a speech impediment.
- Rahab was a prostitute.
- Jeremiah was too young.
- Elijah was suicidal.
- Jonah ran from God.
- The woman at the well had been divorced several times.
- Zacchaeus was very short.
- Timothy had a stomach problem.
- Lazarus was dead.

God chooses ordinary people with issues. We would have chosen differently. We would have based our choice on looks, skills, and acquired education (Doctor of Theology, Doctor of Divinity). We would look for the brightest and the most gifted.

How to Fight Your Enemy

You might think that you don't have any enemies, but everyone has enemies, whether they're completely innocent or not. Even if you're a good person who hates conflicts, there will be people out there who will hate you and who will want to see you suffer.

Everyone is going through some kind of despair, some kind of struggle, and they aren't even aware that it's because of their enemy. The sickness you're going through is not there by itself; the financial problem is not there by itself. The depression, the frustration, the family problem, the problem at church, your troubled relationship... none of these exist on their own. Bet you never thought of that.

The sister that hates you, the jealous person, your boss or supervisor who's always on your back... they are not your enemy. The first step to successful spiritual battle is knowing your enemy. What—or whom—are you fighting?

The Bible says: *"For we wrestle not against flesh and blood, but against principalities, against powers, against the rulers of the darkness of this world, against spiritual wickedness in high places,*" (Ephesians 6:12). We're talking about the prince of the air, a high ranking demon, and well organized forces of darkness. Unfortunately, he's invisible and very evil. No matter what you do, you can never please this enemy. He is pure evil. You can't make deal with this enemy. You can't negotiate, bargain, or argue logically with him. He's irretrievably and irrevocably evil. He's invisible, evil, and on the attack. The Bible says that he's like a roaring lion, seeking whom he may devour.

The second step in fighting the enemy is knowing who you are. This includes knowing the source that you are connected to.

The third step is to know and understand your weapons. Understand that the weapons of warfare are not carnal, but mighty in pulling down every stronghold.

The Whole Armour
Most importantly, you have to be strong in the Lord, meaning that you need a relationship with God, and you must be in union with God. You have no strength outside of God. It's your relationship with God that make you strong. You draw spiritual strength from God. You can't put on the whole armour if you don't have a relationship with God.

How Do You Fight When the Enemy Comes at You?
The enemy wants you to experience regret and remorse, but not repentance. Your defense is Jesus Christ, who is interceding on your behalf. We need to turn to Him in faith, deny our pride, and conquer the enemy by surrendering to God. Satan will accuse you, but do not listen. Turn to Jesus Christ, your advocate, and confess your sins to Him.

One of Satan's names in the Bible is "Accuser." Satan wants to make you think you are the worst Christian ever. Some of you have listened to his accusations for so long, you actually think that they're true. Satan lies to you and says, "If you told anybody about that, they would hate you." He wants to silence you; he wants to isolate you. The last thing he wants is for you to come out into the light and taste the grace of confession, repentance, forgiveness, and healing.

You may start to doubt God's goodness. When Satan came to Eve in the Garden of Eden in his original attack against humanity, he said to her: "You know why you can't have that fruit? It's because God knows that you'd become like Him, and He's just cutting you a raw deal." See what a lie that is against the character of God?

You begin to doubt the goodness of God when you start saying, "I don't know why I'm the only one who has these physical struggles. I don't know why I'm the only one who has this financial challenge. I don't know why I have to be the only one who has a spouse who is this demanding and difficult; I don't know why I should have kids who don't turn out the way I had hoped." Satan will hand you self-pity like candy.

Satan is the master of lies and deceit. Jesus said of Satan, *"There is no truth in him,"* (John 8:44). When he lies, he's just speaking his native language, because he's the father of lies. Satan says to you, "Oh, that sin is going to be fantastic." And you know what? It's not as fantastic as he says it will be. He says that God's not there, and that you haven't overcome that sin yet, so you might as well just stop trying. When you start to follow his lies and choose some of those things that you know are foolish and selfish, you end up making a junkyard of your old age. You sit there amidst the twisted wreckage of ruined relationships and horrible choices, and Satan will mock you.

You may feel a strong impetus to separate from other Christians. The Bible says, *"Let not the sun go down upon your wrath: neither give place to the devil,"* (Ephesians 4:27). When you and I are hurt by another believer and we nurse that wound and harbour unforgiveness, we give the devil a foothold in our life. Maybe Satan gets to your through doctrinal issues. You may think to yourself, *If I have to tell somebody off over it, I will. If I have to leave this church over it, I will. Because what really matters here is this issue—and I'm right on this issue!* You may end up right on that issue—but you also end up harder, colder, and isolated.

Your Defense: The Indwelling Spirit of God
Pride is a strong weapon, and Satan is a strong adversary. Only a stronger power can give us the victory. That power comes from the Holy Spirit of God.

If thine enemy be hungry, give him bread to eat; and if he be thirsty, give him water to drink: For thou shalt heap coals of fire on his head, and the Lord shall reward thee.
—Proverbs 25:21-22

"*Submit yourselves therefore to God. Resist the devil, and he will flee from you,*" (James 4:7). Unless you know your enemy, he will always win.

Do Good to Those Who Hurt You

Jesus repeats a command found throughout the Bible: show mercy to your enemies. When you show mercy to your enemies, you rise above them, instead of sinking down to their level.

If you love those who love you, what credit is that to you? For even sinners love those who love them ... But love you enemies, and do good, and lend, expecting nothing in return; and your reward will be great, and you will be sons of the Most High; for He Himself is kind to ungrateful and evil men. Be merciful, just as your Father is merciful.
—Luke 6:32, 35-36, NASB

Jesus said:

Truly I tell you, whatever you bind on earth will be bound in heaven, and whatever you loose on earth will be loosed in heaven. Again, truly I tell you that if two of you on earth agree about anything they ask for, it will be done for them by my Father in heaven. For where two or three gather in my name, there am I with them.
—Matt. 18:18-20, NIV

Know your enemy and know yourself, and you can fight a hundred battles without disaster.

A "sweet enemy" refers to a person you hold close but who most likely will stab you in the back at some time. He/she may appear innocent, carefree, and overly lovely, but if you look closer, you might see the bad eyes and the cold stare, and you may even catch a cold breeze from his/her breath. Sweet enemies have a reason for being close to you—simply to destroy or harm you. It's often difficult to discover that these people actually mean harm, but they do.

22. IDENTIFYING A CULT CHURCH

THE VERY CHURCH THAT WE ATTEND COULD BE A CULT CHURCH. How do we identify one? In order to witness effectively, to impart, to give wisdom and understanding to the followers, we must first know how cults work—their techniques, why people join them, and how to come out of a cult. Cults are any groups who deviate from biblical teaching in any form. We can identify a cultic church in a variety of ways.

- They put themselves on an equal level with Christ.
- Leaders extol their superiority over others.
- Leaders present themselves as being God's chosen ones, and claim that through them great blessings will flow, especially to their followers.
- The leaders claim that there is no one in this world who is more powerful than them.
- Leaders instill fear into their followers in order to control.
- Cult leaders can be very charming. They will praise you because they are experts at pretending to be loving and are very convincing.
- They will prey on your weak areas in order to lure you.
- They claim to be the only one with new insight into God's plan and purpose.
- The leaders will claim that God has revealed things to them that He has never revealed to anyone else.
- They claim to be more spiritual than anyone else.

- Leaders do not allow their followers to grow spiritually.
- Leaders refuse to provide certain biblical teaching to their followers so they can be enlightened with "the truth."
- Leaders don't allow their followers to participate in other Christian activities or even visit other Bible-believing churches.
- Leaders restrain their followers from making independent, spiritual, and rational decisions.
- Leaders induce guilt with confusion and self criticism in their followers.
- If you are not in agreement with the leader, the church tells you that there must be something wrong with you. You must agree with the leader, even if you are agreeing with sin.
- Regardless of all the other churches, they claim that their church is the one true church.
- They will announce that if you leave their church, something bad will happen to you.
- Leaders often tell their followers that they are not growing, while at the same time telling them that they are very powerful, have special gifts, and are even more spiritually mature than anyone else.
- One day they will often openly embarrass you, and the next praise you in secret.
- The leaders make every decision for you, so the growth of the followers is stifled.

Why Is it Hard to Leave a Cult?

- When you're in a cult, you're in an extended family.
- You find instant love and friendship that will disappear upon leaving them.
- The leaders keep the followers so busy with events and activities within their organization that they will become too busy even to think for themselves.

- The followers often are like robots, because they are brainwashed.
- The leaders usually work on their followers' emotional, psychological, and social needs.
- Their followers are often living in fear and intimidation.
- Unless the Holy Spirit opens the spiritual eyes of those who are under the cultic spell, they will not even believe that they are in a cultic church.
- Followers feel fear of rejection, fear of the unknown, obligation, pride, and confusion.

How to Leave a Cult

- Run for your life.
- It's necessary to leave once you're convinced that you are in a cult and are violating God's will. However, that's easier said than done. It can be very hard to come out, but where there is a will, there is a way.
- In order to come out, you must first choose whom you will serve—man or God?
- Seek support from other Christians.
- Associate with godly people and those who will give you godly counsel, encouragement, love, and care.
- Ask God to take you out and adhere to His leading.
- Give no indication to the cult leaders or other followers that you are aware that they are a cult and that you are planning to leave.
- Understand that Christ is the one responsible for your salvation and that no man can give you the salvation that Christ gives.

Why Do People Join Cults?

- lack of knowledge of the Word or God
- a sense of belonging

- human need to part of a group or community
- the need for acceptance
- searching for love
- searching for truth
- the enemy has deceived them, blinding their eyes to the truth
- searching for emotional stimulation
- love being entertained
- love self-gratification
- financial, emotional, and social needs
- seeking for safety and security
- a sense of loyalty
- sometimes low self-esteem
- desire to have others to make decisions for them
- looking for purpose
- naivety

If you are in a church and you recognize that it's a cult, I beg you to run for your life before it's too late. Not only will this involvement compromise your salvation, but it will take away your joy, peace, and blessing in Christ. It will also cause you to lose your soul to eternal damnation.

23. TEACHING OUTLINE FOR BABY CHRISTIANS

WHAT IS A TEACHER? A TEACHER IS ONE WHO HELPS SOMEONE ELSE TO LEARN. In other words, the teacher cooperates with the students in learning. He doesn't seek to perform before an audience made up of listening students, but he undertakes with them in an activity in which they are busily engaged. There is no teaching unless there is learning. The teacher has not really taught unless the student has learned. The object of our teaching is to make something happen in the lives of our students. The test of our teaching is what happens in the lives of our students.

Topics

1. Grace and Mercy: We are Saved through God's Grace

- Romans 6:23: *"For the wages of sin is death, but the gift of God is eternal life in Christ Jesus our Lord,"* (NIV). All of us are sinners deserving of death, but grace comes to us in our poor sinful condition and offers us the mercy of God when we deserve His wrath. Mercy occurs when God withholds the punishment we deserve because of our sinfulness. The consequence of sin is death, yet Jesus paid this penalty for us. If it wasn't for God's mercy, you would not be here. We are deserving of judgment, destruction, punishment, and condemnation.

- Ephesians 2:8: "*For by grace are ye saved through faith; and that not of yourselves: it is the gift of God.*" Grace is the unearned gift the Father gives to His children. The Lord relates to us by His grace. Grace has provided salvation to all who come to Him, even though we deserved destruction. God knew that the man He created would sin.
- Psalms 111:4: "*He hath made his wonderful works to be remembered: the LORD is gracious and full of compassion.*"
- Psalm 136:1b: "*His mercy endureth forever.*"
- Second Corinthians 12:9a: "*My grace is sufficient for thee: for my strength is made perfect in weakness.*"
- Romans 3:24: "*Being justified freely by his grace through the redemption that is in Christ Jesus.*"
- Titus 3:7: "*That being justified by his grace, we should be made heirs according to the hope of eternal life.*"

2. Love: You are Loved by God

- John 3:16: "*For God so loved the world, that he gave his only begotten Son, that whosoever believeth in him should not perish, but have everlasting life.*"
- Romans 5:8: "*But God commendeth his love toward us, in that, while we were yet sinners, Christ died for us.*"
- First John 3:1; "*Behold, what manner of love the Father hath bestowed upon us, that we should be called the sons of God: therefore the world knoweth us not, because it knew him not.*"
- First John 4:9-10: "*In this was manifested the love of God toward us, because that God sent his only begotten Son into the world, that we might live through him. Herein is love, not that we loved God, but that he loved us, and sent his Son to be the propitiation for our sins.*"
- First John 4:12; "*No man hath seen God at any time. If we love one another, God dwelleth in us, and his love is perfected in us.*"
- First John 4:14: "*And we have seen and do testify that the Father sent the Son to be the Saviour of the world.*"

3. Forgiveness: You Are Forgiven of Your Sins by God through Jesus Christ

- First John 1:9: "*If we confess our sins, he is faithful and just to forgive us our sins, and to cleanse us from all unrighteousness.*"
- Daniel 9:9: "*To the Lord our God belong mercy and forgiveness, though we have rebelled against him.*"
- Matthew 26:28: "*For this is my blood of the new testament, which is shed for many for the remission of sins.*"
- Mark 1:4: "*John did baptize in the wilderness, and preach the baptism of repentance for the remission of sins.*"
- Luke 24:47: "*And that repentance and remission of sins should be preached in his name among all nations, beginning at Jerusalem.*"
- Acts 2:38: "*Then Peter said unto them, Repent, and be baptized every one of you in the name of Jesus Christ for the remission of sins, and ye shall receive the gift of the Holy Ghost.*"
- Acts 26:18: "*To open their eyes, and to turn them from darkness to light, and from the power of Satan unto God, that they may receive forgiveness of sins, and inheritance among them which are sanctified by faith that is in me.*"
- Ephesian 1:7: "*In whom we have redemption through his blood, the forgiveness of sins, according to the riches of his grace.*"

4. Baptism: What is the Significance of Baptism?

- John 3:36: "*He that believeth on the Son hath everlasting life: and he that believeth not the Son shall not see life; but the wrath of God abideth on him.*"
- John 5:24: "*Verily, verily, I say unto you, He that heareth my word, and believeth on him that sent me, hath everlasting life, and shall not come into condemnation: but is passed from death unto life.*" The Scriptures tell us that we believe first and then we are baptized. Baptism does not save anyone.

- What does "baptized for remission of sins" mean? It means union with Jesus. The Apostle Paul speaks of being united with Him by baptism (Romans 6:5). *"For all of you who were baptized into Christ have clothed yourselves with Christ,"* (NASB). *"Then Peter said unto them, Repent, and be baptized every one of you in the name of Jesus Christ for the remission of sins, and ye shall receive the gift of the Holy Ghost,"* (Acts 2:38).
- Romans 6:3-4; Colossians 2:12. The Bible also refers to baptism as a symbol of dying to the old life and burying it when the believer goes down under the water. When he or she comes up out of the water after baptism, the Bible likens it to rising from the grave with Christ to a new life.
- Acts 22:16: *"And now why do you wait? Rise and be baptized and wash away your sins, calling on his name."*
- Romans 6:1-4. Baptism is an outward sign of an inward commitment. Water baptism is our way of showing what has happened inside our hearts.
- First Corinthians 12:13: *"For by one Spirit are we all baptized into one body, whether we be Jews or Gentiles, whether we be bond or free; and have been all made to drink into one Spirit."*

5. Prayer: Jesus' Model Prayer for Believers

- Matthew 6:5-9. How to and how not to pray. Those who pray with wrong motives will receive their rewards; likewise, those who pray with right motives will also receive their rewards.
- Matthew 6:9. To whom should we pray? Jesus said we are praying to *"Our Father."* God is the Father in that He is the Creator of all mankind. He is also a caring Father who provides both physically and spiritually (Matthew 5:45, 6:33). We have access to our heavenly Father. We

are not praying to a natural father, but to a supernatural father, a divine father, an everlasting father. He is Father of us all.

- Matthew 6:9. How do we approach God in Prayer? "*Hallowed be thy name.*" He is a holy God. When we go before Him, we need to respect Him, revere Him, and honour Him; this is a time to give Him the praises He deserves. This is also a time to repent of our sins before Him.
- Matthew 6:11. What we should ask for in prayer? "*Give us this day our daily bread.*" We might be at the bottom of our resources and have no one to help us, but God will provide for us if we ask Him. "Bread" in this passage is not referring to the things we want in life, but the things we need (Matthew 4:4). Jesus taught us to take life one day at a time. Many problems can be solved if we focus on "today" instead of last week, yesterday, or tomorrow. Through prayer, we can ask for our daily needs and He will supply all our needs according to His riches.
- Matthew 6:12. Forgiveness through prayer. Jesus said, "*And forgive us our debts.*" All are sinners, even Christians (Romans 3:23; 1 John 1:8-10). No matter how bad our sins are, in prayer we can ask God to forgive us of all our sins. Confession of sin is required (1 John 1:7). There are, indeed, conditions to receiving forgiveness. We must ask in faith, ask unselfishly, and ask in a state of obedience (James 1:6; 1 John 3:22). Another condition is that we forgive our debtors. Jesus explained, "*But if ye forgive not men their trespasses, neither will your Father forgive your trespasses,*" (Matthew 6:15).
- Matthew 6:13. Praying about temptation. We are faced with temptation every day, but if we ask God in prayer, He will lead us into all truth; God has promised that His children will be provided a way of escape.

6. Healing: We Can Receive Healing through Jesus Christ

- Isaiah 53:5: "*But he was wounded for our transgressions, he was bruised for our iniquities: the chastisement of our peace was upon him; and with his stripes we are healed.*"
- 1 Peter 2:24: "*Who his own self bare our sins in his own body on the tree, that we, being dead to sins, should live unto righteousness: by whose stripes ye were healed.*" Note: Jesus died for both our sins and our sicknesses. Our healing is in Jesus Christ through His atoning sacrifice. We are already healed.
- Matthew 4:23-24: "*And Jesus went about all Galilee, teaching in their synagogues, and preaching the gospel of the kingdom, and healing all manner of sickness and all manner of disease among the people. And his fame went throughout all Syria: and they brought unto him all sick people that were taken with divers diseases and torments, and those which were possessed with devils, and those which were lunatick, and those that had the palsy; and he healed them.*" Note: Jesus has power to heal "every disease and sickness." There are no limits to healing.
- John 4:49-51: "*The nobleman saith unto him, Sir, come down ere my child die. Jesus saith unto him, Go thy way; thy son liveth. And the man believed the word that Jesus had spoken unto him, and he went his way. And as he was now going down, his servants met him, and told him, saying, Thy son liveth.*"
- James 5:14 "*Is any sick among you? let him call for the elders of the church; and let them pray over him, anointing him with oil in the name of the Lord.*"
- Notes: Healing is ministered to people; people can be healed through the spoken word. They can also be healed through the laying on of hands, prayer, and anointing of oil by the elders.

CONTACT INFO FOR SPIRITUAL HOSPITAL

Phone: 416-526-0763

Email: info@spiritualhospital.ca

Facebook: www.facebook.com/spiritualhospital/

Youtube: www.youtube.com/channel/
UCf6cN-PQrncnC3d32qHDEZQ

Web Site: www.spiritualhospital.ca